Creating Instructional Capacity

Creating Instructional Capacity

A Framework for Creating Academic Press

Joseph Murphy

CORWIN
A SAGE Company

FOR INFORMATION:

Corwin

A SAGE Company

2455 Teller Road

Thousand Oaks, California 91320

(800) 233-9936

www.corwin.com

SAGE Publications Ltd.

1 Oliver's Yard

55 City Road

London EC1Y 1SP

United Kingdom

SAGE Publications India Pvt. Ltd.

B 1/I 1 Mohan Cooperative Industrial Area

Mathura Road, New Delhi 110 044

India

SAGE Publications Asia-Pacific Pte. Ltd.

3 Church Street

#10-04 Samsung Hub

Singapore 049483

Executive Editor: Arnis Burvikovs

Associate Editor: Desireé A. Bartlett

Editorial Assistant: Andrew Olson

Production Editor: Amy Schroller

Copy Editor: Erin Livingston

Typesetter: C&M Digitals (P) Ltd.

Proofreader: Laura Webb

Indexer: Amy Murphy

Cover Designer: Anupama Krishnan

Marketing Manager: Maura Sullivan

Printed in the United States of America

ISBN 978-1-4833-7456-7

This book is printed on acid-free paper.

SUSTAINABLE FORESTRY INITIATIVE

Certified Chain of Custody
Promoting Sustainable Forestry
www.sfiprogram.org
SFI-01268

SFI label applies to text stock

15 16 17 18 19 10 9 8 7 6 5 4 3 2 1

Contents

Preface

For the last 35 years, my colleagues and I have been studying school improvement in general and the cardinal role of leadership in helping schools to improve in particular. We continue that work here by examining leadership of the instructional program. Building great schools is about two tasks: creating productive culture and creating instructional capacity. In our last book, *Creating Productive Cultures in Schools* (2014), we examined one of those two pillars in considerable detail. Here, we turn the spotlight on the second pillar, the instructional capacity.

In Part I, we establish the general storyline of school improvement. The first chapter in Part I examines the larger political, economic, and social forces in the nation that shape school improvement and provide understanding about the nature of school improvement leadership. Chapter 2 takes us backstage in the school improvement play. We see a good deal of the critical dimensions of school improvement that are often "backgrounded" in the work of change and reform. Surfaced here, they are then threaded throughout the remaining chapters of the book.

In Part II of the book, we review the central role of vision in school improvement. In Chapter 3, we peer deeply into the role that school leaders play in improving schools by examining the three ingredients of vision: mission, goals, and expectations. In Chapter 4, we provide the map for how school improvement leadership works, with a special focus on the critical role of leaders in promoting powerful school cultures and creating a powerful academic press.

In Part III, we zero in on leadership of the instructional program. Chapter 5 addresses the critical role that school leaders play in staffing schools and providing and allocating material resources. We then turn in Chapter 6 to an analysis of leadership in the broad domain of talent development.

The final part of the book carries us further into what we call *school as academic place*. As is the case throughout the book, the focus is on the second pillar of highly productive schools, *academic press*. In Chapter 7, we explore the essential norms from which academic press grows—or the norms that define academic press. We close Chapter 8 with a detailed analysis of how leaders need to approach and manage curriculum and assessment in their schools.

About the Author

 **Joseph Murphy** is the Frank W. Mayborn Chair at Vanderbilt's Peabody College of Education. He has also been a faculty member at the University of Illinois and The Ohio State University, where he was the William Ray Flesher Professor of Education.

In the public schools, he has served as an administrator at the school, district, and state levels. His most recent appointment was as the founding president of the Ohio Principals Leadership Academy.

He is past vice president of the American Educational Research Association and was the founding chair of the Interstate School Leaders Licensure Consortium (ISLLC). He is a Fellow of the American Educational Research Association.

His work is in the area of school improvement, with special emphasis on leadership and policy. He has authored or coauthored twenty-three books in this area and edited another twelve. His most recent authored volumes include *The Educator's Handbook for Understanding and Closing Achievement Gaps* (2010), *Homelessness Comes to School* (2011), *Leadership Lessons for School Leaders* (2011), *Homeschooling in America* (2012), *The Architecture of School Improvement* (2013), and *Creating Productive Culture in Schools* (2014).

He led the development of the ISLLC Standards for School Leaders in 1996 and the subsequent revisions. He is one of the four creators of the Vanderbilt Assessment of Leadership in Education (VALED).

Dedicated to Richard "Pete" Mesa and William L. Bainbridge

PART I

Understanding School Improvement

1

Shaping Forces

A central tenet of our scholarship over the years is that school improvement and school improvement leadership must be viewed in terms of how schooling is evolving and the forces that are driving those changes. For us, therefore, a decontextualized understanding of school improvement leadership is insufficient. Our models inform us that both the understanding of leadership and the practice of leadership need to backward map from knowledge about the type of schooling needed in a postindustrial world. This, in turn, necessitates, among other things, an understanding of the economic, cultural, and sociopolitical environment in which schooling is nested.

This chapter explores the evolution of schooling from the industrial world (1880–1990) to the current technological era (1990 to present). As we will see, the scaffolding on which schooling in the 20th century was built is crumbling. New pillars required to meet new values and goals are being framed up. Whether this reconstruction work is productive will depend in large part on leadership.

We begin by providing an overview of the model that guides our analysis of change in schools over the last 125 years. We then show how one major revolution produced an understanding of schooling that defined the practice of education throughout the industrial era. We close by exposing the tenets of a second revolution currently underway, one that is forming our understanding of schooling in the postindustrial world of the 21st century. And to make the point one more time, it is this understanding on which school improvement and school improvement leadership are built.

A MODEL OF ORGANIZATIONAL EVOLUTION

Over the last half century, scholars have invested considerable energy in the quest to uncover answers to the question of how industries and organizations evolve, devoting special attention to the influence of external movements on the shape and functioning of institutions. In the mid-1980s, in an effort to bring coherence to this work, Tushman and Romanelli (1985) crafted their seminal theory of *organizational evolution*, the punctuated equilibrium model of organizational change. At the core of their model, Tushman and Romanelli hypothesize that "organizations progress through *convergent* periods punctuated by *reorientations* which demark and set the bearings for the next convergent period" (p. 173). According to the theory, *convergent* periods cover long time spans during which incremental and marginal shifts that refine and elaborate organizational elements (e.g., goals) toward increased alignment dominate. *Reorientations*, on the other hand, encompass "periods of discontinuous change where strategies, power, structure, and systems are fundamentally transformed toward a new basis of alignment" (p. 173).

In short, industries and organizations within them tend to go along for extensive periods of time with only marginal changes. Then, for reasons explored below, they get pushed out of their orbits. At these times, fundamental changes are needed to ensure organizational success.

According to the model, it is external shocks to the system that necessitate radical change (transformation), shocks that punctuate change. Researchers in this field maintain that these disturbances arise from social, legal, cultural, ecological, political, economic, and technological shifts in the environment. For example, technological shifts are forcing newspapers and magazines to leave well-established routines and seek out new foundations on which to build in much the same way that afternoon newspapers found it necessary to adapt (unsuccessfully) to significant cultural shifts in the environment in the 1960s and 1970s. Researchers also conclude that a sustained period of poor performance can induce disturbances that demand transformation.

THE INDUSTRIAL ERA
OF SCHOOLING: WHERE WE WERE

Change Forces (1890–1920)

As just noted, prolonged poor performance is one of the two forces that provide the fuel to cause institutional disequilibrium, to push organizations out of well-established operational orbits. Moving into the 20th century, there was a widespread and growing feeling that the system of schooling of the 19th century was in trouble. On the one hand, because the center of gravity for the institution was preparation for college, enrollments were quite low and schooling was failing to address the needs of the majority of students who were not planning on attending college. In short, schooling at the turn of the 19th century was not educating the great bulk of America's youngsters and was preparing almost no one "for life."

Equally important, schools were seen as failing society—in particular, the rapidly emerging industrialized society. By and large, because the socialization and skill sets needed to function in the new economy were not being provided, schools were seen as out of step with needs of a post-agrarian society. Nor were they providing much help in dealing with the problems accompanying the mass immigration of the time.

According to Tushman and Romanelli (1985), environmental shifts provide the axis on which major institutional changes are scaffolded, especially significant alterations in the ambient social, political, and economic contexts impacting an industry. On the political front, the change with the greatest impact on education as we moved into the industrial era was the rise of progressivism and the development of the liberal democratic state. Rooted in discontent with political corruption and an expanded recognition of government as too limited for the new industrial era, the political landscape was noticeably recontoured in the late 19th and early 20th centuries. Direct citizen control and machine politics began to give way to bureaucratized institutions led by a cadre of educational experts.

The social tapestry was also being rewoven during the period from 1890 to 1920. The central dynamic was "the transformation of American society from one characterized by relatively isolated self-contained communities into an urban, industrial nation" (Kliebard, 1995, p. 2). Industrialization and demographic changes were reshaping the nation. Most important from our perspective here is the fact that these shifts in social conditions resulted in significant changes in schools. As Cremin (1961), Kliebard (1995), Tyack (1974), and Wraga (1994) have all demonstrated, "[w]ith the recognition of social change came a radically altered vision of the role of schooling" (Kliebard, 1995, p. 1).

Turning to the economy, we see the emergence of new economic realities brought on by the industrial revolution. At the core of the matter was the transformation from an agricultural to an industrial economy—or, perhaps more accurately, given the social changes outlined above, to an industrial society. The nation was witnessing the "advent of machine production and its accompanying specialization of occupation" (Koos, 1927, p. 310). Stated in language that eerily would be reintroduced nearly a century later in reshaping the school to the realities of a postindustrial world, it could be said that by 1890 "national concerns about international economic competition" (Spring, 1990, p. 220) and the demands of "advancing technology" (Krug, 1964, p. 209) began to influence the design of the blueprints being used to shape the foundations of the newly emerging model of education.

Convergence (1920–1990)

The period between 1890 and 1920 began with the publication of one of the most important reports on education ever produced in the United States—the 1893 *Report of the Committee on Secondary School Studies*, commonly referred to as the *Report of the Committee of Ten*—and ended with the publication of another—the 1918 report from the National Education Association titled *Cardinal Principles of Secondary Education*. It was a time when the learning and teaching foundations that defined comprehensive schooling for nearly a century were poured. It was here that the educational response to the new industrial world that would define the 20th century was forged. More specifically, it was during this era that the ideology that would define schooling was developed and implanted in education. We pull the strands of this shifting ideology into three clusters: core values and purpose, technical core, and organizational architecture and governance.

Core Values/Purpose

Although public education started out as a practical endeavor, by the end of the 19th century, it was dominated by college interests. Preparation for college largely determined what was taught. Agreement on the central aim of public education was short-lived, however. By 1920, the purpose of schooling would be radically redefined.

In their famous 1893 report, the Committee of Ten attempted to resolve the question of purpose by "merging the high school's two functions into one" (Herbst, 1996, p. 109). The eerily current perspective of the Committee was that there was no difference in these two aims and that preparation for life should lead naturally to preparation for college. As Cremin (1955) and others have highlighted, it was the Committee's belief in the primacy of "improving intellectual ability by disciplining the mind" (p. 297) that allowed them to arrive at this resolution: "The best preparation for life was to strengthen the intellect. . . . The discipline-centered college preparatory curriculum was viewed as the program best suited for all youth" (Wraga, 1994, p. 2). Practical knowledge, they held, would come later from work and everyday life.

Analysts have concluded that "the report of the Committee reflected the crossroad between an educational system designed to provide everyone with a common education and an educational system organized to provide everyone with a specific education based on a future social destination" (Spring, 1990, p. 200). The signals provided by the committee—that the purpose of education was to develop the mind—pointed schooling in a direction that urban, industrialized America of the 20th century was unwilling to follow: "The Committee had in fact written an epitaph instead of a blueprint for the future" (Herbst, 1996, p. 108). "The Committee did not see the vast scope of the issues facing American schools and thus did not prescribe for them in any way. As a result, the suggestions in the *Report* became obsolete within two decades" (Sizer, 1964, p. 170).

Those who believed that the aim of education was intellectual development were not able to hold the high ground. Between 1890 and 1920, a new agenda—education for social control—buttressed by a new science of learning known as *social efficiency*, gradually came to dominate education. This newly forming purpose rested on a rejection of what critics believed to be an outdated view of schooling. According to many analysts of education during the early years of the 20th century, "Intellectual development was of course vital, but it had to be reconciled with the school as a social institution and its place in the larger social order" (Kliebard, 1995, p. 54).

Subject to the pull of the environmental conditions described earlier, a focus on individualism began to give way to the social purposes of schooling. The dominant leitmotif was that of schooling as a mechanism of social control. Social efficiency, in turn, became the central concept in influencing the reconfiguration of schooling.

Education for social control included the introduction of new ideas (such as specialization) and a reformulation of older ones (such as equality of opportunity). It represented a rejection of the prevailing position on the academic function of education and provided an affirmation of the practical aims of schooling. It acknowledged the role of the school in addressing new socially anchored responsibilities. Analysts argued that "educational functions traditionally carried on by family, neighborhood, or shop [were] no longer being performed; somehow they must get done; like it or not, the school must take them on" (Cremin, 1961, p. 117). Social efficiency meant fundamentally that the function of schools would be to prepare students for the new industrial world that was redefining American society—for what Spears (1941) called "the great and real business of living" (p. 56). Advocates of the new goal of social control "wanted education to produce individuals who were trained for a specific role in society and who were willing to work cooperatively in that role" (Spring, 1990, p. 201).

The Technical Core of Schooling

The period from 1890–1920 was marked by "a vigorous drive to replace what was commonly regarded as a curriculum unsuited for the new industrial age and for the new population of students entering . . . secondary school in larger numbers" (Kliebard, 1995, p. 156). One change was that academics would be illuminated much less brightly than they had been before the turn of the century. As the belief that schooling was too academic became ingrained in the American culture, the curricular spotlight was redirected elsewhere.

As the academic scaffolding supporting schooling in the 19th century was dismantled, a new infrastructure rose up to take its place—one constructed more from the raw materials of personal and practical experiences than from the frameworks of the academic disciplines. Practical education was required and the opportunity for employment took on added significance. *Schooling for life* was no longer education for college but rather preparation for a job. When social control as the foundation for schooling and social efficiency as the theory of learning became dominant threads in the tapestry known as education, a diminished— and continually decreasing—role for academics would also be woven into the fabric.

The pieces that complete the pedagogical aspect of industrial-era schooling focus on the organization of the curriculum and on student access to subject matter. Students would no longer be educated alike, with similar (or at least equivalent) curricular experiences. Instead, a number of new ideas would emerge to help reground the curriculum and to shape the variety of learning experiences available to students. One of these perspectives grew directly from the incipient body of knowledge being codified by child development psychologists. Indeed, although not quite pushed into ascendancy, the belief in the student as the axis of the school curriculum was advanced during this era. This viewpoint maintained "that children, not books and teachers, ought to be the schools' starting place" (Powell, Farrar, & Cohen, 1985, p. 261) and "that the child's own natural impulses could be used as a way of addressing the question of what to teach" (Kliebard, 1995, p. 37).

A second perspective, *social efficiency*, would hold even greater influence over the organization of the curriculum during the development of schooling for the industrial era. Like their colleagues who saw adolescent needs as the appropriate ground for curriculum development, social efficiency advocates clamored for greater variety in the learning menu. Unlike their colleagues, however, they saw the landmarks on the new curricular frontier defined not by individual interests of students but by societal needs and goals. Students were viewed not as individuals but as members of groups. Subject matter would be organized in different bundles to be parceled out to students in these varied groups. As Kliebard (1995) documents, "Predicting future destination as the basis for adapting the curriculum to different segments of the school population became a major feature of curriculum planning" (p. 13) during the period from 1890–1920. What was called for was education that matched young people to appropriate work roles.

Organizational Architecture and Governance of Schooling

The revolutionary changes that took root in education from 1890 to 1920 were not confined to vision and learning and teaching. The methods used to govern education and the designs employed to structure schools also underwent significant alterations, which were in directions heavily shaped by the powerful political, social, and economic currents outlined above. The defining element of the organizational revolution was the shift from lay control, which dominated the governance landscape before 1890, to a "corporate bureaucratic model" of governance (Tyack, 1974, p. 6). As was the case in the construction of the learning infrastructure, the new scientific models of school organization and governance provided some of the defining components of education for a post-agrarian world.

The organizational transformation that marked the evolution of education was laced with two central ideologies, a "corporate form of external school governance and internal control by experts" (Tyack, 1974, p. 146). Both elements drew freely from models supporting the development of the post-agricultural business sector. "Working under the banner of the depoliticalization of schooling and eliminating political corruption, reformers sought to remove the control of schools as far as possible from the people" (p. 167) to eliminate community control. As was the case with the development of the differentiated curriculum, the struggle to separate education from politics was powered in part by both antidemocratic ideology and class prejudice. In terms of influence, we know that this movement accomplished much of its goal. By 1920, throughout the nation, a closed system of governance that would dominate education for the next 75 years had replaced much of the more open system that had prevailed at the end of the 19th century.

Shifts in the basic governance equation during the early decades of the 20th century were accompanied by a reconfiguration in the way schools were managed and structured. One distinctive development was the appearance of a class of administrative experts to whom government agents delegated control for the management of schools. Borrowing from the new models of organization and management being forged in the corporate sector, reformers began to develop analogs between the leadership of business enterprises and the management of schools. They argued that to reform education, power needed to be concentrated at the top.

In order to facilitate the use of this centralized power and to maximize its potential to effect change, reformers drew up blueprints for a new structure for their institution (bureaucracy) and cobbled together a new philosophy of leadership (scientific management), borrowing freely from materials originally crafted in the corporate sector. In so doing, they brought forth the array of operating principles that would form the organizational backbone for schooling throughout the 20th century, principles such as authority vested in office, differentiation and specialization of roles, professionalism, separation of management from labor, chain of command, and so forth.

POSTINDUSTRIAL SCHOOLING: THE CURRENT VOYAGE

Change Forces

Sense of Failure

As we entered the 1990s, the foundation of schooling that had stood for nearly three quarters of a century had begun to show significant deterioration. There was a widespread feeling that schools were performing poorly. Crosnoe (2011) hit the mark directly when she reported that "these are definitely not the glory days of the American educational system" (p. 3). What analysts saw as frustration over the continuing inadequacies of education in the United States was a multifaceted phenomenon. Or, stated in an alternate form, the perception that the level and quality of education in schools is less than many desire was buttressed by data on a wide variety of outcomes. Specifically, critics argued that data assembled in each of the following performance dimensions provided a not-very-flattering snapshot of the current performance of the American educational system: (1) academic achievement in basic subject areas—compared to student performance in other countries; (2) functional literacy; (3) preparation for employment; (4) the holding power of schools (dropout rates); (5) knowledge of specific subject areas such as geography and economics; (6) mastery of higher-order skills; and (7) initiative, responsibility, and citizenship.

Two issues in particular tied in analyses of educational outcomes at the turn of the 20th century: (1) the inability of the educational enterprise to enhance levels of productivity to meet the needs of the changing workforce and (2) the failure of schools to successfully educate all of the nation's children, especially the poor. While analysts acknowledge that student achievement has remained fairly stable over the last quarter century, they fault education for its inability to keep pace with the increasing expectations from a changing economy.

One side of the problem critics discuss is the belief that systems that hold steady in today's world are actually in decline. While others see stability, they see damaging obsolescence. The other side of the productivity issue raised by these reviewers is the claim that because of the changing nature of the economy, the level of outcomes needed by students must be significantly increased. They find that the schools are not meeting this new standard for productivity. Complicating all of this is the knowledge that high levels of performance must be attained by nearly all of society's children.

What appears to be especially damaging to public education at the current time is the perceived inability of schooling to reform itself. Questions raised by analysts who take the long-term view on this issue are particularly demoralizing. What has resulted from reform efforts, critics argue, has not been an increase in educational quality but rather a proliferation of professional and bureaucratic standards, the creation of subsidies for bureaucracy, a widening gap between professional educators and the general public, and the strengthening of a centralized educational system that disadvantages taxpayers and parents. Beers and Ellig (1994) make this point in a dramatic fashion when they claim that "in a very real sense we have tried to run the public schools the same way the Soviets tried to run factories, and now we're paying the price" (p. 20). The effect, critics maintain, is that reform has reinforced the very dynamics that are promoting self-destruction in education. The natural consequence, they hold, must be the emergence of new forms of educational institutions.

Changing Environment

At the same time, and consistent with the Tushman and Romanelli (1985) model, American education finds itself in a roiling environment of economic, political, and social changes. To begin with, it is almost a fundamental law that the economy is undergoing a significant metamorphosis. There is widespread agreement that we have been and continue to be moving from an industrial to a postindustrial or information economy. Key aspects of the new economy include the globalization of economic activity, the demise of the mass-production economy, a privileging of information technology, an increase in the skills required to be successful, and an emphasis on the service dimensions of the marketplace. The ascent of the global economy has brought an emphasis on new markets and cracks in the model of public monopoly.

Along with these changes, as we discuss below, have come increasing deinstitutionalization, deregulation, and privatization of the American system of education. There is a growing belief that markets offer more hope than the public sector. There is a new spirit of market-based entrepreneurship in play.

The political and social environments also are undergoing important changes. There has been a loosening of the bonds of democracy. The infrastructure of civil society also has been impaired. As a consequence of these basic shifts—the weakening of democracy and the deterioration of civil society, especially in conjunction with the ideological space that they share with economic fundamentalism—important sociopolitical trends have emerged. One strand of this evolving sociopolitical mosaic is plummeting public support for government. In many ways, Americans "have disengaged psychologically from politics and governance" (Putnam, 1995, p. 68). As Hawley (1995) chronicles, "Citizens are becoming increasingly alienated from government and politics. They do not trust public officials" (p. 741) and they are skeptical of the bureaucratic quagmire of professional control that defined education for almost all of the 20th century.

At the same time, many analysts have explored the accelerating movement toward a society marked by great wealth and great poverty.

According to Dahrendorf (1995), this economically grounded trend represents a new type of social exclusion. He and others are quick to point out that this condition seriously undermines the health of society: "Poverty and unemployment threaten the very fabric of civil society. . . . Once these [work and a decent standard of living] are lost by a growing number of people, civil society goes with them" (pp. 25–26).

Consistent with this description of diverging life chances is a body of findings on the declining social welfare of children and their families. These data reveal a society populated increasingly by groups of citizens that historically have not fared well in this nation, especially ethnic minorities and citizens for whom English is a second language. Concomitantly, the percentage of youngsters affected by the ills of the world in which they live (for example, poverty, unemployment, illiteracy, crime, drug addiction, malnutrition, poor physical health, and homelessness) is increasing.

Convergence

Across the last quarter century, we have argued that a new convergence has emerged in the American schools, one that parallels in scope the changes seen in that institution from 1890–1920. Three central alterations are visible: (a) at the technical level, a change from teaching to learning and a change from transmission to social-constructivist views of learning; (b) at the organizational level, a change from bureaucratic and hierarchical systems to more communal views of schooling; and (c) at the institutional level, a rebalancing of the governance equation, one that adds more weight to market and citizen control while subtracting influence from government and professional elites. Below, we examine these changes.

The Core Technology

As we discussed above, from the onset of the industrial revolution, education in the United States has been largely defined by a behavioral psychology-based model of learning—a model that fits nicely with the bureaucratic system of school organization in play during the last century. This viewpoint in turn nurtured the development of the factory and medical practice models of instruction that dominated schooling throughout the 20th century. Under these two models, the belief that the role of schooling is to sort students into the able and less able—those who would work with their heads and those who would work with their hands—became deeply embedded into the fabric of schooling.

What is important here is that the current period of upheaval just reviewed has placed us "in the midst of redefining, even recreating conceptions of learning and teaching in schools" (Prestine, 1995, p. 140); a shift in the operant model of learning is a fundamental dynamic of the current struggle to redefine education. The behavioral psychology-based model that highlights the innate capacity of the learner has been challenged by notions of constructivism and situated learning and by the components of authentic pedagogy. As Prawat and Peterson (1999) inform us,

> Social constructivism represents more than an addition to the traditional, individualistic perspective that has dominated research on learning for most of [the 20th] century. It . . . represents a dramatically different approach to learning, requiring fundamental changes in how . . . educators think about the process. (p. 203)

Under this approach to learning, schools that historically have been in the business of promoting student adaptation to the existing social order are being transformed to ensure that all youngsters reach ambitious targets of performance.

The Organizational Architecture

For some time now, "critics have argued that the reforms of the Progressive Era produced bureaucratic arteriosclerosis—and the low productivity of a declining industry" (Tyack, 1993, p. 3). There is an expanding feeling that the structure of schooling that was hardwired into the system between 1890 and 1920 and that has dominated education ever since has outlived its usefulness. In particular, it is held that the management tools of the bureaucratic paradigm pull energy and commitment away from learning. Reformers maintain that the structure cemented in place during the first recreation of schooling between 1890 and 1920 is not capable of supporting excellence in education and that, even worse, bureaucratic management has actually been damaging learning.

It is also argued that bureaucracy has led to stand-alone, singled-out schools, that the structure that defined 20th-century schooling is counterproductive to the needs and interests of educators in postindustrial schools. In particular, these reviewers find that the existing structure is incompatible with a professional orientation. They maintain that the hierarchical foundations laid during the reform era (1990–1920) of the industrial period have neutered teachers and undermined "the drawing power and holding power of strong collegial ties" (Little, 1987, p. 502). These reviewers contend that "it has become increasingly clear that if we want to improve schools for student learning, we must also improve schools for the adults who work in them" (Smylie & Hart, 1999, p. 421).

As might be expected, given this tremendous attack on the basic organizational structure of schools, stakeholders at all levels are clamoring for significant reform, arguing that the bureaucratic framework of school organization needs to be rebuilt using different blueprints and materials. There is widespread agreement that the top-down, authoritarian approach to leadership has taken us about as far as it can. There is a significant demand for new ways of organizing schools, especially in the way they are led.

New perspectives of education feature these new methods of organizing and managing schools. In the image of schools for the 21st century, the hierarchical bureaucratic organizational structures that have defined schooling since the early 1900s are giving way to systems that are more focused on capacity building and are more communal.

In these redesigned, postindustrial school organizations, there are basic shifts in roles, relationships, and responsibilities: Traditional patterns of relationships are altered; authority flows are less hierarchical—traditional distinctions between administrators and teachers begin to blur; role definitions are both more general and more flexible—specialization is no longer held in such high regard; because influence is based on expertise, leadership is dispersed and is connected to competence for needed tasks as well as formal positions; and independence and isolation are replaced by cooperative work. Furthermore, the traditional structural orientation of schools is overshadowed by a focus on the human element. The operant goal is no longer maintenance of the organizational structure but rather the development of human resources. Building learning climates and promoting organization adaptively replaces the more traditional emphasis on uncovering and applying the one best model of performance. A premium is placed on organizational flexibility and purpose and values.

A new model for school leadership acknowledges that shared influence strengthens the organization. Institutional perspectives no longer dominate the organizational landscape. Rather, schools are reconceptualized as communities, professional workplaces, and learning organizations. Professional community-oriented conceptions that challenge historical bureaucratic understandings of schools as organizations move to center stage. Ideas such as community of leadership, the norms of collaboration, inquiry communities, and the principle of care are woven into the fabric of the school organization. The metaphor of the school as community is brightly illuminated.

Institutional Dynamics

Some analysts of the institutional level of schools—the interface of the school with its larger (generally immediate) environment—argue that the industrial approach to education led to a privileging of government and a "cult of professionalism" (Sarason, 1994, p. 84) and to the "almost complete separation of schools from the community and, in turn, discouragement of local community involvement in decision making related to the administration of schools" (Burke, 1992, p. 33). Critiques of extant governance systems center on two topics discussed extensively above: (1) frustration with the government-professional monopoly and (2) critical analyses of the basic governance infrastructure—bureaucracy.

Many chroniclers of the changing governance structures in schools envision the demise of education as a sheltered government monopoly dominated by professionals. As noted above, in its stead, they forecast the emergence of a system of schooling driven by economic and political forces that substantially increase the saliency of market and democratic forces. Embedded in this conception are a number of interesting dynamics. One of the key elements involves a recalibration of the locus of control among levels of government, an idea known simply as *localization* or, more commonly, *decentralization*. However it is labeled, it represents a backlash against the centralized and bureaucratic form of education and governance of the industrial era of education.

A second ideological foundation can best be thought of as a recasting of democracy, a replacement of representative governance with more populist conceptions, especially what Cronin (1989) describes as *direct democracy*. While we use the term more broadly than Cronin does, our conception of the solidifying convergence here shares with his a grounding in (1) the falling fortunes of representative democracy, a "growing distrust of legislative bodies . . . [and] a growing suspicion that privileged interests exert far greater influence on the typical politician than does the common voter" (p. 4), and (2) recognition of the claims of its advocates that greater direct voice will produce important benefits for society.

A third foundation encompasses a rebalancing of the control equation in favor of lay citizens while diminishing the power of the state and (in some ways) educational professionals. This line of ideas emphasizes *parental empowerment*. It is, at times, buttressed by a strong strand of anti-professionalism that underscores citizen control and local involvement.

The ideology of *choice* is a fourth pillar that is also rebuilding linkages between the school and parents and community stakeholders. Sharing a good deal of space with the concepts of localism, direct democracy, and lay control, choice is designed to open up both the demand and supply side of markets.

CONCLUSION

We find that schools are generally resistant to and able to deflect and accommodate reform efforts during the long stretches of time when previously turbulent economic, political, and social environments have cooled and activity domains have hardened. No matter how hard reformers hammer education during these periods of convergence, change occurs on the margins, if at all.

On the other hand, there is also considerable evidence that the hard equilibrium that defines American education is indeed subject to destabilization and reforming. It does seem to require considerable energy to punctuate the status quo, however. In particular, change depends on major and overlapping strands of environmental pressures. In the last two centuries, we have seen these conditions appear twice. One occurred as the

19th century turned into the 20th and schools changed to respond to the perceived needs of an industrial economy and a post-agrarian web of politics and culture. The second arose as the 20th century melded into the 21st and education began its struggle to recast itself as consistent with the political, social, and economic DNA of an information society. The essential elements in the domains of activity that came to define the periods of convergence that preceded and followed the first era of turmoil were documented above. In addition, our understanding of the cardinal dimensions and elements that will define postindustrial education were described. It is the latter set of changes that define schooling and establish the frames for school leaders today. In Chapters 2 and 3, we continue our discussion of the broad storyline of school improvement. In Chapters 4 through 8, we look deeply into one of the two essential aspects of leadership for school improvement: leading the instructional program.

2

School Improvement: The Backstage Story

S chool improvement is mainly about the "stuff" that needs to be addressed. Over the years, the "goods" have been called *correlates*, *factors*, *elements*, *ingredients*, and so on. This book is about the instructional program dimension of the school improvement narrative, what we refer to as *academic press*. But it is also about conditions and supports that both link elements and provide some of the fuel for them to work well (e.g., cohesiveness). Appropriately, we illustrate these threads of the school improvement story throughout the chapters on the instructional program (Chapters 4–8). In this chapter, because leadership for school improvement requires a clear understanding of and ability to work with this knowledge, we pull these conditions and supports from the background and put them on center stage. We start with some guidelines about the road to school improvement and move on to analyses of core-supporting concepts such as context and coherence. It is important to begin with an acknowledgment that there is considerable overlap among these supports and conditions.

Major figures in the study of organizational change and school improvement have described the school improvement pathway as uneven and full of unexpected twists and turns. Scholars in these domains portray change as evolutionary as well as planned. The voyage, according to Ancess (2003), is marked by "a pattern of fits, starts, retreats, and starts again rather than as a smooth linear path" (p. 32).

In particular, analysts have discovered that school improvement work is often characterized by increased tensions, the unsettling of comfortable routines, cultural resistance, new enactments of micropolitical behavior, and the surfacing of legitimate concerns. Thus, they document that change is often accompanied by an implementation dip. Things are likely to trend downward, both in human terms (such as confidence and morale) and performance before they turn upward.

Relatedly, we learn that success is fragile. Victory is hardly inevitable and, once garnered, requires some vigilance to maintain. Turnover of personnel is often accompanied by regression. Energy naturally leaks out of the system, and the loss is often unnoticed or, if detected, not replenished. The environments in which schools find themselves are always evolving, pushing one reform forward only to be replaced by another a short time later. Mandates proliferate, overload sets in, fragmentation increases, meaning dissipates, and people withdraw to the safety of the past and the comforts of old routines. Change becomes a ritual that washes over the school. Sustainability is undermined.

MULTIFACTOR WORK

One of the most important understandings that has emerged from the broad field of school improvement, especially improvement for students placed at risk, is that troubles and problems are traceable to the broader society in which schools are nested. Therefore, school improvement efforts must extend beyond the school. This means collective work. To start, it means a larger role for nonschool agencies in reshaping the political, economic, and cultural forces that disadvantage many children. Second, it suggests that schools and other institutions and systems of support need to work in tandem. None alone are likely to be successful, especially when improvement means turning around troubled situations. Third, it necessitates greater efforts on the part of schools to extend their work beyond the traditional boundaries of schooling, to take ownership for a wider array of services.

We have also learned over the years that there is no single factor, element, or component that will lead to dramatic school improvement. What is required is a collective attack, "a mix of strategies" (Thompson, 2002, p. 5). A productive school improvement design would be comprehensive, providing a combination of elements. It would provide significant initiatives on a number of fronts (i.e., be multilayered and multitiered). As we discuss in detail below, the design would be interconnected, aligned, integrated, and coordinated. It would feature what Miller (1995, p. 376) calls the principle of "complementarity" at both the strategy and institutional levels. It would attend to both the short and long term. It would offer redundancy.

The chronicle on multistranded school improvement work contains a number of key subthemes. We know, for example, that there are some components that are necessary not because they push the needle forward but because their absence can derail the rest of the bundle of work. A safe and orderly learning environment falls into this category.

We also know that weaknesses in any of the key pieces of the overall design make improvement problematic; each element needs to reach at least the moderate level of effectiveness. Additionally, there is some evidence of a multiplier effect in play. *A* may be weak by itself, as might *B*. Together, however, they might produce a moderate to strong effect, what Hattie (2009) refers to as an *interaction effect*. It is a combination of small effects working together that make a difference.

Studies of school improvement with nearly every group of students at risk inform us that the more disadvantaged the population, the more effort is needed to reach success and the more constant that work must be. For example, while middle-class school communities benefit from school improvement ingredients measuring at mid-level strengths, only high strength leads to improvement in at-risk communities.

Researchers have also uncovered another dimension of the multiple factor law. Both academic and cultural levers need to be engaged. As Becker and Luthar (2002) remind us:

> Methods that demand higher educational standards without a similar emphasis on the social-emotional needs of early adolescents will not result in much success, efforts to improve the social-emotional needs of disadvantaged students without a comparable application of instructional and curricular methods to attain academic excellence will be similarly ineffective. (pp. 204–205)

Clearly, then, "instruction matters and it matters a lot; but so does the social context in which it is embedded" (Bryk, Sebring, Allensworth, Luppescu, & Easton, 2010, p. 209). Indeed, "the greatest achievement effects follow from strong combinations of communality and academic press" (Shouse, 1996, p. 47).

There is emerging evidence that the multifactor package of school improvement components must not pivot solely on remediation. Successful work requires simultaneous movement on helping youngsters catch up and keeping them in sync with their classmates. An effective design needs to include both remediation and acceleration. The corollaries are that (1) early intervention efforts almost always trump later work and (2) prevention of problems trumps remediation of problems.

Some of the most important sub-lessons threaded into the work of school improvement address issues of time. We learn, for example, that sufficient time to get reforms germinated is quite important. We also learn from research that it takes considerable time for improvement initiatives to flower. An analog in this story is that, in general, improvement is developmental; it appears gradually and incrementally. Schools by and large do "not make dramatic improvements, but rather incremental improvement over time" (Huberman, Parrish, Hannan, Arellanes, & Shambaugh, 2011, p. 9).

Success is by no means assured in the school improvement game, especially when situations and environments are turbulent and when schools are in troubled conditions. Because of this, and for substantive and symbolic reasons, small wins over time are heralded in the school improvement literature. These small impacts are often quite meaningful. An important but less developed time theme is that some interventions play out differently across the career of students. For example, teacher expectations carry more weight with younger students. Other time themes were noted previously; early is better than later and prevention trumps remediation.

SEEDBEDS

Perhaps the most essential law that leaders need to burn into their minds is that structural changes do not predict organizational outcomes: "[S]tructural change changes structure, not substance" (Ancess, 2003, p. 140). Numerous studies have affirmed this fact over the last quarter century in nearly every domain of schooling, and nearly every school leader has been frustrated by this truth. Additionally, what holds for structures holds for resources and policies as well. This is particularly unsettling knowledge because leaders have been inculcated to rely on structural change to power reform. Additionally, for reasons that Elmore (1995) explains in his classic essay (i.e., ease of use and high symbolic value), policy makers and other reformers routinely perpetuate the logic and practice of structural change.

Four lines of explanation shed light on the disconnect between structure and school improvement. One focuses on the fact that structures are a long way from outcomes: "[T]he path between macro-level reconfigurations and micro-level processes and activities is long, many-jointed, and loosely linked in a number of places" (Murphy, 1991, p. 76). Structures need to produce changes in the conditions of learning if they are to be successful. However, it is a problematic bet that they can do so. For example, moving from a regular schedule to a blocked one does nothing to change the quality of instruction nor the robustness of the curriculum in classrooms. Advisory periods are as likely to be sterile as they are to foster personalization.

A second line of analysis concludes that schools are characterized by deep patterns of who they are and how they do the business of education. Structural patterns that are inconsistent with the existing grammar of schooling routinely fail to produce desired change. The *existing conditions*, if you will, almost always cause new ideas to conform to the prevailing ideology rather than to shape it.

Third, there is considerable evidence that structural changes are often introduced with little sensitivity to the local context or situation in the school, regardless of whether or not there is congruence with the prevailing climate. We examine this problem in more detail in the following section.

Finally, schools are generally subject to the mistaken belief that the "goods" they want to import are an integral part of the structure they are inviting in (e.g., "community" always accompanies changes in the size of a school). The problem is that the assumption is false. The result is that the structure is imported but the DNA that made it work elsewhere is not. Schools end up with structural shells—empty forms—that do not power school improvement.

The great paradox here is that while reworking the climate, or the *seed-bed*, of the school is the main work, structural changes are required to hold new patterns and understandings in place. That is, while structures have only limited influence on conditions that enhance learning, without them, new perspectives will dissipate.

CONTEXT

School improvement sleuths examining every aspect of change arrive at the conclusion that regardless of the reform agenda context is a cardinal but not determinate variable in the school improvement equation. Context helps set the rules and norms as well as the constraints that shape improvement work. Because situations are idiosyncratic, reforms must be molded to fit the context at hand.

To begin with, it is important to remember that district context can heavily influence school-based improvement work—for better or worse. Relatedly, a massive amount of evidence has accumulated that community contexts create powerful forces that can bolster or hinder improvement initiatives. Socioeconomic status, ethnicity, language, housing conditions, location (urban/rural), history, and so forth all matter.

Hattie (2009), in his hallmark meta-analysis, documented that classroom contexts exert considerable pull over improvement efforts as well. Teachers bring their own cultural understandings, skills, and backgrounds to the job. Each develops a grammar of instruction that impacts how he or she views and engages with change. The importance of the teacher as "person-in-context" (Ford, cited in Geijsel, Sleegers, Leithwood, & Jantzi, 2003, p. 232) is an important theme that is often overlooked in conducting school improvement work. For example, investigators often report that younger teachers with fewer years of experience are more apt to actively engage in reform efforts. Subject matter taught and department affiliation also have a role in this narrative.

School context also influences the viability and meaningfulness of improvement efforts, both directly and through the way it shapes activities in classrooms and the sensemaking of individuals. We know, for example, that grade level often produces different interpretations of change efforts. Geographical location has been found to be influential. So too has the health of the school and the extent of the challenges it confronts (that is, where it falls on the continuum from troubled to highly effective). Lack of enrollment stability or high student mobility also shapes school improvement efforts. Because youngsters from different environments view education and schooling in different ways, demographics of the student body are regularly uncovered as a school-level contextual variable that influences school improvement work. The nature of the community of adults in the schools is also consequential, especially the nature of relationships in place.

The fact that context matters, and that it matters a good deal, has implications for school leaders. We begin with some caveats. To maintain that context is important is not the same thing as arguing that it is determinate, and understanding acknowledgment does not require principals to be held hostage to context. Also, to underscore the importance of the situation does not mean that generalized school reform ideas are dead on arrival. Indeed, as Leithwood (2005) reminds us, "[L]eadership practices are common across contexts in the general form but highly adaptable and contingent in the specific enactment" (pp. 620–621). Or, turning to Bryk and associates (2010), "the most effective managerial form for an organization is contingent on the technical and environmental circumstances affecting the core work of the organization" (p. 67). Thus the notion that all school reforms need to be completely homegrown is scientifically unjustified. The objective is flexibility to meet or adapt to local conditions.

At the same time, leaders need to acknowledge the place of situation in school improvement work, to understand that reform does not "occur in a vacuum, devoid of its surrounding context" (Coldren & Spillane, 2007, p. 18). Included here is the understanding that what works easily or smoothly in one school may require the investment of considerable capital and energy in another school. It also means acting in ways that honor the limitations of telling and mandating as engines of school improvement. Improvements have to play out at the street level. While the prize is never abandoned, localization and customization are needed (and appropriate) to gain it. Strategies must be formed to fit the situation while working simultaneously to influence context in directions that support improvement. To be sure, the process cannot be permitted to produce "lethal mutations" (Penuel, Fishman, Yamaguchi, & Gallagher, 2007, p. 931) of reforms, but adaptation will be the norm. Leaders also need to be cognizant of the fact that this adaptive school improvement work is likely to produce unintended consequences.

COHERENCE

Building on the findings from the pioneers in the effective schools movement, we distilled consistency, coordination, integration, and alignment (i.e., coherence) as the four essential beams supporting successful improvement. This conclusion has been affirmed on a regular basis over the last 20 years. More importantly, analysts peering in on successful practices have unearthed the dimensions or essential aspects of coherence:

- integration within each component of school improvement work
- alignment across subject areas (e.g., a single point of view about writing across all academic domains)
- integration between and among components of the work (e.g., between mission/goals and professional development)
- coordinating the four pieces of the instructional program—standards, instruction, curriculum, and assessment
- working as a collective rather than as a discrete set of individual actors
- abandoning practices and policies that get in the way of improvement or that foster fragmentation and overload
- keeping the core issues at the center and maintaining a ferocious focus on what counts
- shaping influences from beyond the organization (e.g., the state, the community) to fit the school's context and goals
- cascading improvement efforts and values across organizational levels (e.g., district, school, classroom), not isolating them to a single area
- employing resources in an integrated manner, especially personnel
- getting organizational policies, structures, operating systems to operate in tandem and in mutually reinforcing ways (e.g., around time usage)
- building redundancy into improvement work
- aligning the formal and informal aspects of the organization
- filtering discordant messages and demands
- shaping the sensemaking frames that hold the high ground in the school
- linking short- and long-term perspectives
- thoroughly compressing variability in the academic program and the school culture
- integration between school and work

We close our discussion of alignment and coordination with a few important reminders. It is the principal who is the prime actor in the coherence narrative, the one who wields the tools to forge integration. For a variety of reasons, coherence is not a natural state in schools. Things are more likely to pull apart than cohere. Alignment, integration, and cohesion require a strong hand.

CAUTIONS

Some important guidance in the area of school improvement attends to costs. One guideline reminds us that the reforms that have the greatest power to drive improvement tend to be the most costly, too. At the same time, because these costs often do not require new outlays of funds (e.g., people already on the payroll are shifted to new responsibilities), these costs often go uncounted. Third, reliance on additional external resources generally does not work well for long-term improvements. Finally, it is necessary that benefits not be the sole criterion of helpfulness or impact. School leaders need to remember that interventions have both benefits and costs. And while it is often difficult to isolate the impact of particular interventions, "[c]onsiderably more effort than is now the norm needs to be devoted to assessing both of these dimensions of reform efforts and trying to determine the ratio between the two, to determine where efforts are most cost effective" (Barton, 2003, p. 37).

We also have discovered that it is difficult to predict the exact consequences of improvement efforts. As reported earlier, the fact that the school improvement road is bumpy, reciprocal, nonlinear, and jumbled makes this nearly inevitable. We also know now that unintended consequences, both good and bad, find their way into school improvement endeavors, what Leithwood (2008) describes as "collateral outcomes" (p. 18). One message for leaders is that they need to spend some time working on these consequences. The unplanned for can often be foreshadowed with some effort and insight. Another message is that leaders need to be prepared to deal with these consequences, both in advance and after they arrive on the scene.

CONCLUSION

In the first chapter of this introductory part of the book, we examined the broad forces that shape school improvement. Here, we turned the spotlight on the embedded threads in the school improvement tapestry. In the second part of the book, we look at school improvement leadership globally. We begin with an in-depth analysis of the critical variable of *vision*.

PART II

Leadership for School Improvement

3

Vision
With Daniela Torre

W e learn from the broader literature on leadership that vision routinely surfaces in studies of effective organizations. We see this logic
in studies of school improvement and of the leaders in improving schools.
School success and vision for learning are empirically linked. As we discuss throughout the book, vision is especially critical in periods of major
transitions in education.

Researchers also report that the principal is generally the essential figure in ensuring that a school vision is created. Or, in alternate form, vision
focus distinguishes more effective from less effective principals. It is hardly
surprising, then, that vision is a hallmark component of every important
school leadership framework, beginning in the 1980s.

We unpack vision into three distinct but related domains: *mission*,
which addresses overarching values and purpose; *goals*, which provide
direction; and *expectations*, which establish specific targets. All three seem
to be required for vision to impact student learning.

CREATING MISSION

At the broadest level, vision is about moral purpose and possibilities, concepts forged from values and beliefs on which school improvement is scaffolded. As Fullan (1982, 1993, 2002) has reminded us numerous times,

mission is the bedrock of school improvement. Schools do not progress well without it. Additionally, mission rarely evolves without the guiding hand of the principal.

Researchers have also harvested important clues about how mission serves school improvement. Mission influences the instructional program and the learning climate, which in turn shape the behaviors of teachers and students. Because schools are loosely coupled systems, they often lack clear goals. In such situations, there is a natural tendency for effort to splinter, an effect only exacerbated by the frenetic nature of schooling. Mission begins to tighten systems by establishing the boundaries in which schooling occurs. Mission coheres means and ends around shared values and beliefs.

It is important to note that not all school missions harness equal amounts of energy. From our analysis, we have distilled eight core values that anchor stronger missions, those that consistently direct the school into productive channels of work (i.e., school improvement). To begin with, the mission needs to convey a sense of hope, to open the door of possibility. Missions should be inspirational. They need to convey a palpable sense that conditions (e.g., low levels of success, disaffiliation) are malleable and that improvement is possible, even likely.

In addition, missions should address commitment to success and to the effort that such commitment entails. This encompasses the understanding that second best is insufficient and the conviction that the school can and will improve. In a related vein, mission should reflect the belief that all students will be successful. That is, no one is permitted to fail. The embedded understanding is that schooling is the game changer for students, a conviction and moral imperative about success.

Relatedly, mission should reflect asset-based thinking about students and the larger community. As Edmonds (1979) and Brookover and colleagues (1977, 1978, 1979) reported at the beginning of the modern era of school improvement, this third core idea pushes back against the deficit-based thinking often found in struggling or failing schools and schools with large numbers of students placed at risk. It is anchored on the belief that all students are capable of learning, that the school does not underestimate the abilities and efficacy of children. *Asset-based thinking* means not accommodating instruction to preconceived assumptions of limitations but rather conducting schools in ways that change students' abilities and interests. Optimism rather than pessimism holds the high ground. Problems and failure are not attributed to children and their families. Deficiencies are not assumed. Negative attitudes are conspicuous by their absence. Constraints are recognized but they are challenged as impediments to success. Schools push back on resistance to norms of success proactively, not reactively.

Student focus is the fourth core element/value in mission. Student-centered values hold the high ground. The spotlight is on children and youth, what is in the best interests of students. Effective leaders run child-centered schools. Concretely, that means developing structures, policies, operating systems, and budgets around a learner-centered ideology and the specific youngsters in the school.

Fifth, the mission in improving schools is academically anchored. It highlights student learning and academic success. An academically focused mission targets the instructional program. Teaching and learning hold center stage and better instruction is the primary job.

Effective leaders also develop outcome-focused missions. These outcomes feature measures of student learning in general and provide markers of student achievement in particular. Seventh, missions in effective schools carry the value of continuous improvement. Norms of complacency are challenged. Risk taking is promoted, and there is an appetite for change. Finally, missions in improving schools are characterized by a norm of collective responsibility. A culture of accountability emerges, replacing traditions of externalizing responsibility. Success is a collective endeavor.

ESTABLISHING GOALS AND EXPECTATIONS

Goals

Five storylines in the area of school goals merit attention. To begin with, goal setting is seen as one of the most influential roles that principals can undertake to promote school improvement. Second, schools are often found to have vague goals, ones that lack the power to direct action, especially teacher behavior. Third, even when there are clear goals, they are often developed in ways that do not encourage ownership by school staff. Fourth, schools that are effective in helping all students reach ambitious targets of performance have widely shared and clearly formed academic goals, goals that are "both a property of leadership and a quality of school organization" (Robinson, Lloyd, & Rowe, 2008, p. 659). Fifth, in getting goals right, considerable attention needs to be devoted to the content of the goals as well as the goal development process. We explore both of these issues—content and processes—below.

Nature of the Goals

Our analysis of research over the last 35 years leads us to conclude that goals that function well can be identified by critical markers. The most essential of these is a focus on the academic domain in general and on student learning in particular. We know that goals are most productive when they are specific, not generic. Supovitz and Poglinco (2001) make this point as well, concluding that while generic goals can be a starting point, the "exponential value of instructional leadership comes from a marriage of intensive organizational focus on instructional improvement with a clear vision of instructional quality" (pp. 3–4). Barnett and McCormick (2004) call this a *task focus* and Strahan (2003) refers to it as a specific *stance about learning*. Thus academic focus and learning stance are essential. They positively impact student achievement.

Implicitly and explicitly, other cardinal elements can be discerned in an analysis of academic learning focus. We discover, for example, that goals are best managed when the spotlight is on students, when there is a student-first perspective, and when student achievement is the central theme. Researchers also inform us that the goals that are found in improving schools are challenging but achievable and apply to all students. They direct activity but are not rigid. Goals that work well are meaningful to school staff. Meaningfulness includes knowledge of, internalization of, and ownership of goals.

Almost every study of leadership for school improvement has concluded that goals need to be clear and concrete, not abstract or subject to interpretation. They should provide stakes in the ground, indicating the destination and the way to travel. Parsimony and simplicity are desirable. Scholars also report that goal clarity in improving schools directs the allocation and development of human and financial resources. Recent studies have also identified the importance of tailoring goals to context (the specific needs of students in a given school at a given time). Short-term goals that move the school to larger ends are desirable as they permit staff to experience reinforcing, short-term wins. It is important, however, that these short-term wins derive from and support the more encompassing mission of the school.

Developing and Communicating Goals

Analyses across time also reveal important insights about the ways in which effective schools forge goals. One critical discovery is the importance of a process that fosters staff ownership of goals. The literature highlights both the personal engagement of the principal and collaborative work of teachers here. What is particularly important is the creation of ownership of the work to reach goals and responsibility for the results of those efforts. Wide participation of community stakeholders and reliance on hard data to arrive at decisions also define goal development in high-performing schools.

School improvement leadership is also about ensuring that school goals are important; importance is nurtured by discussing and reviewing goals with staff periodically during the school year, especially in the context of instructional, curricular, and budgetary decisions. Both formal communications (e.g., goal statements, staff bulletins, articles in the principal or site-council newsletter, curricular and staff meetings, parent and teacher conferences, school handbooks, assemblies) and informal interactions (e.g., conversations with staff) are used to communicate the school's mission.

Not only do effective leaders spend more energy than their peers in communicating goals, they also appear more successful in getting their messages through. For example, researchers conclude that teachers in schools with robust school improvement leadership are more aware of and can clearly communicate the school's mission and goals. Their counterparts in schools with less effective instructional leadership lack a common understanding of schoolwide goals and expectations.

The emerging theme from the research runs as follows: The development and inculcation of widely shared, ambitious, and unambiguous learning goals is one of the most valuable instruments in the school improvement toolbox. We close this part of our analysis with a note on what that research tells us about how goals function to fuel school improvement. At a fundamental level, goals adhering to the description above provide tangible meaning to the school mission. In so doing, they solidify action around shared values and purpose. They signal importance to all stakeholders. As such, they help people see more clearly. They keep staff from becoming distracted by separating the really important work from the balance of activity. Effort becomes more focused and more productive. Goals also serve as a powerful mechanism for organizational cohesion, helping leaders with the essential role of coordinating action in complex organizations.

On the personal side, strong goals can be powerful motivators for staff, encouraging educators to reach for higher standards. Goals have been shown to have an energizing effect. They also have the potential to bring about cooperative work and to help dismantle the wall between teaching and school administration. Shared work, in turn, can strengthen commitment and responsibility.

Expectations

Expectations are the third layer of school vision. They make even more concrete the understandings of performance for members of the school community. They create a platform to bring goals to life. They are both a measure of and a method to develop academic press and productive culture in the school.

Over the last four decades, researchers have shown that expectations have important organizational consequences. Most importantly, they differentiate between more and less effective schools, with higher academic expectations linked to better outcomes, outcomes defined in terms of student learning. They work in part by helping to shape school culture and by promoting organizational learning. Expectations have their largest impact on children on the wrong side of the achievement gap, especially children from low-income families.

On the teacher front, expectations help define in concrete terms under-standings of quality. According to Leithwood, Jantzi, and Steinbach (1999), who have examined this issue in considerable depth,

> expectations of this sort help teachers see the challenging nature of the goals being pursued in their school. They may also sharpen teachers' perceptions of the gap between what the school aspires to and what is presently being accomplished. Done well, expressions of high expectations also result in perceptions among teachers that what is being expected is also feasible. (p. 69)

High expectations convey in tangible fashion the hard work required to create a school where all youngsters reach ambitious targets of performance. They can energize faculty to work collectively, assume leadership responsi-bilities, and keep student improvement in the spotlight. At the heart of the success equation here are consistency and repetition of shared expectations.

VISION IN ACTION

Operationalization: The Possibilities

So far, we have constructed a scaffold for school vision, one highlighting three domains: mission, goals, and expectations. Our remaining assign-ment is to review the research on how leaders help keep vision vibrant and at the center of school improvement work. We know that schools are shaped by context and are highly complex and deeply human enterprises. They are also layered over with a wide assortment of demands from a diverse array of stakeholders. Under these conditions, it is not unusual for vision to fall by the wayside or to lose its directive power. Vision often becomes simply another item on an extensive list of important things. A meaning-infusing tool is transformed into a "bureaucratic necessity" (Leithwood et al., 1999, p. 60). The specific implications for work are often undeveloped. Even when they are forged, they often go missing.

> Because considerably more happens in schools than the pursuit of explicit goals, even the most goal-focused leaders will need to skill-fully manage the constant distractions that threaten to undermine their best intentions. Such distractions, in the form of new policy initiatives, school crises, calls for goal revision or abandonment, and the need to maintain school routines that are not directly goal related, all threaten to undermine goal pursuit. (Robinson et al., 2008, p. 667)

Thus we know that considerable effort is required to keep vision in a starring role, to ensure that "the mission serves constantly as the criterion and desideratum for everything" (Raywid, 1995, p. 70). For this to occur, the school needs to go beyond developing mission, goals, and expectations—beyond articulation, that is. Everyone needs to be committed to the vision. The staff, with the principal on point, needs to refresh and reinforce school vision, consciously working to maintain it as a driving force. Trust is a key leavening agent in most school matters but never more so than in building commitment to the school's mission, goals, and expectations for children. Trust is central to Timperley's concept of "vision in action" (2009, p. 220).

As was the case with the formulation and dissemination of vision, the principal's actions are critical in bringing vision to life and to keeping it healthy. Leaders' actions foster the commitment of others, nurture needed workplace trust, and steer improvement work—or not. Or, as Kruse, Seashore Louis, and Bryk (1995) so aptly note, "What leaders say and do expresses what they value for the organization, and the behavioral expectations that they communicate on a daily basis either reinforce or call into question these basic values." (p. 39)

Elsewhere we have made the empirical case that forging consistency, coordination, coherence, and alignment is one of the two or three most critical cross-domain functions of school leaders. Given the truism that "you get what you work on in schools" (Louis & Miles, 1991, p. 77), nowhere is that responsibility more essential than in the operationalization of school vision, pushing, pulling, and carrying vision into the workflow of the school. We know that in more effective schools, vision acts as the "organizing principle" for work (Desimone, 2002, p. 451). Vision encourages aligned actions in the service of school improvement. It becomes infused into key organizational activities such as operating procedures, structures, policies, and budgets and is the cardinal leitmotif of school culture. Challenges are addressed and problems attached less on an ad hoc basis and more within the guidance of a master roadmap. As a consequence, there is less organizational drift and better uptake of organizational values.

Communicating and Consensus Building

Beginning with the studies on school and teacher effects in the 1970s, investigations have been adding to our understanding of how leaders work to operationalize vision. Two themes from our analysis—consensus building and communication—were introduced above in our discussion of the goals aspect of vision. We expand on them here. Researchers show us that ongoing, coherent communication around school mission and goals is a hallmark dimension of school improvement. It is, to use a metaphor, the fuel needed to power the school vision. Researchers also unpack the variety of ways communication in the service of operationalizing vision occurs: through (1) the use of stories, symbols, rituals, and slogans; (2) the ways that resources are committed; (3) conspicuous displays of mission, goals, and expectations (including achievements) throughout the school; (4) providing information on mission, goals, and expectations (including news of progress) in all oral and written communications; (5) the clear linkage of vision to educational programs; and (6) acknowledging progress and celebrating success. All of these strategies are enhanced to the extent that the focus is on the specific youngsters in a given school (i.e., that context is taken into consideration).

Earlier, we explained that consensus in mission and goal development promotes a variety of important conditions (e.g., commitment) that mediate school improvement. Here, we deepen that narrative to collective action in operationalizing vision, to ownership of the full staff for school improvement work. Collective work around a shared vision nourishes commitment and efficacy and promotes personal and organizational learning needed to fuel continuous school improvement.

Modeling and Monitoring

Research affirms that leaders infuse vision with meaning by the ways in which they act, by modeling. In effective schools, principals demonstrate commitment with how they allocate their time, where they spend time, what they place on agendas, and how they accept responsibility for school success. They carry the torch for the school and its values, ensuring tight alignment between their behaviors and the school vision. Through modeling, they become catalysts of school improvement.

Colleagues from the earliest studies of school effects have shown the keystone position that monitoring occupies in the improvement algorithm. Here, we highlight its position in relation to the vision dimension of highly productive schools and effective leadership. On that score, there is abundant evidence that rigorous assessment and monitoring of mission, goals, and expectations is an important part of the vision implementation playbook. More importantly, studies reveal that this monitoring occurs in improving schools, but it is not highlighted in reports of stagnant schools. The core elements of this monitoring parallel those found in the general literature on assessment.

CONCLUSION

This chapter on the importance of vision to school improvement was built on three key understandings. First, vision is a hallmark variable in the school improvement algorithm. Second, leadership is the keystone element in developing, implementing, and shepherding the school's vision. This is especially the case for schools in turnaround mode and schools serving high concentrations of students in peril. Third, of all the conditions and ingredients of effective schools, our understanding of vision is the fuzziest. Discussions and analyses of vision often unfold at high levels of abstraction that, while meaningful, provide little direction to researchers, policymakers, developers, and practitioners about how to grasp the concept in ways that can be acted upon—to study, to provide guidance and direction, to forge into tools, and to build, respectively. Our objective in this chapter was to help illuminate this gap and create the blueprint for building a bridge between the abstract and concrete. Thus, we have provided guidance to the four key sets of actors in the school improvement production: researchers, policymakers, developers, and practitioners.

The infrastructure we forged is comprised of three layers: mission, goals, and expectations. Collectively, they direct construction crews to think and work their way to increasingly concrete layers of action but always with the more concrete layers drawing from higher layers of purpose. The framework we employ thus supports one of the most critical laws of school improvement: Consistency and coordination is paramount in the development of effective schools.

Our analysis of the literature allowed us to forge eight specific markers that define mission in highly productive schools: sense of hope, commitment to success, asset-based thinking, student focus, academic anchors, outcome-based focus, continuous improvement, and collective responsibility. We then revealed how goals take form based on these eight core values. We accomplished this by exploring five important storylines we distilled from the research. Finally, we explained how expectations stand in service to goals and, ultimately, to the mission. We closed our treatment of the topic with an analysis of the actions required to bring an integrated and supportive understanding of vision to life.

NOTE

1. This chapter is based on the article "Vision: Essential Scaffolding" appearing in *Educational Management, Administration and Leadership*. It is used with the permission of the journal.

4

School Culture and Academic Press

We define *school improvement* as an increase in effectiveness over time, with effectiveness centered around organizational capacity and the impacts of the deployment of that capacity, especially on student learning. Thus we anchor school improvement in measures of growth or value added. Of course, this leaves the metrics yet to be established, that is, the growth measures and the amount of progress required to be called *improving*.

This book is devoted to what we have referred to over the years as *instructional leadership* or *learning-centered leadership*. Before we drill down on this idea, however, it is helpful to start with an understanding of the broader concept at hand—leadership in general. The essence of leadership is (1) having a sense of where an organization needs to get to or what it needs to achieve and (2) creating the capacity and deploying that capacity to reach desired ends. It is about the process of influencing others, influence exercised through relationships.

Educational leadership is simply the application of these core ideas to schooling: "actions intentionally geared to influence the school's primary processes and, therefore, ultimately students' achievement levels" (Witziers, Bosker, & Krüger, 2003, p. 403). It is this broad definition that is tied in throughout this volume, one that takes an extensive view of the primary processes of schools.

We are abundantly clear throughout the book that *leadership* is not synonymous with *roles*. However, because school administrators are "foundational for instructional leadership" (O'Donnell & White, 2005, p. 56), our focus herein is on how those in formal administrative roles in schools, especially principals, exercise school improvement leadership.

Across time, it has generally been assumed that good leadership is an important force in developing good schools, while poor leadership hinders school improvement. It has only been in the last 40 years, however, that this assumption has been affirmed, beginning with the initial effective schools and instructional leadership studies and continuing through the increasingly sophisticated studies of the last two decades.

Analysts have also been active in documenting the magnitude of that importance, providing concreteness to the influence of leadership as a driver of school improvement. Researchers provide this information from quantitative studies in a variety of ways, most of which are not intuitively clear to practitioners, developers, and policy makers. They employ correlations, effect sizes, months of growth, variance explained, and so forth.

An essential point to remember is that most children's learning is accounted for by nonschool factors such as family conditions and student aptitude. Schooling is responsible for something in the neighborhood of 20 percent of student achievement. So one needs to see whether effects are of all student learning (overall effects) or the part of learning attributable to schools (school effects). For example, if leadership explains 25 percent of school effects, then that is 5 percent of overall impact on student learning.

One also needs to be aware of whether researchers are measuring direct effects of leadership or all effects (i.e., direct effects and mediated or indirect effects). Since, as we will see, most of the impact of principals occurs through their influence on school culture and the instructional program, measures of direct effects are almost always quite low while assessments that include indirect effects are more robust.

On occasion, studies report influence in terms that are more familiar to practitioners. For example, Branch, Rivkin, and Hanushek (2003) use months of student learning as the metric, finding that effective leaders raise achievement levels for students between two and seven months each year while their ineffective counterparts lower achievement by those amounts. Bryk and colleagues (2010) reach a parallel conclusion using growth versus stagnation, as does the Center for Teaching Quality (2007) using growth expectations.

Collectively, through the use of different procedures and tools and employing different metrics, research affirms leadership as an essential variable in the overall equation of student success (i.e., one that includes environmental conditions outside of schooling). That influence is amplified when the school effects-only algorithm is examined and both direct and indirect pathways of influence are included. The summative message is that leadership can and does have significant and meaningful effects on student learning.

As discussed above, we also know that leadership takes on added significance in certain places and in particular times. On the *times* front, we know that leadership becomes more essential when the environment surrounding an institution is roiling. In difficult times, the value and influence of leaders increases as well. So, too, in times of change, especially during fundamental change and on the occasions when the pathway to the future is less than clear. On the *place* front, leadership is more critical in schools with high concentrations of students placed at risk, in low-performing schools, in low socioeconomic status (SES) schools, and in all challenged schools.

Studies over the last 35 years have connected leadership with the effectiveness of most of the major dimensions of education and every important outcome of schooling. On the conditions, variables, elements, or dimensions side of the ledger, there is empirical evidence that effective principals have positive impacts on the following:

- use of technology in schools
- use of data
- instructional practice
- parental/community/school linkages
- staff collaboration
- professional development and organizational learning
- professional community
- staff commitment, trust, motivation, work orientation, job satisfaction, confidence, and accountability
- implementation of reform
- program coherence
- learning climate for students
- academic programs within schools, including special education, vocational education, and bilingual education

On the outcome side of the ledger, effective principal leadership has been shown to influence the following:

- student engagement
- sustainable change
- effective schools
- school improvement
- implementation of large-scale reform
- student learning

The obverse to these storylines is also true, however. Ineffective leadership can negatively impact school conditions and outcomes. Relatedly, leader stability has a role here as well. Leadership continuity is important and change in the principalship often has deleterious effects on the ingredients of quality schooling and the outcomes linked to those conditions.

Before we move more deeply into our exploration of school improvement leadership, a few introductory notes are in order. To begin with, we need to heed the reminder from Leithwood and Montgomery (1982) that "effectiveness is a continuous rather than bipolar condition" (p. 336). While our attention is riveted on leadership, it is important to remember that it is an essential but insufficient element in explaining school improvement and that the ability to attribute cause remains problematic. Within the people domain specifically, there is abundant evidence that others play critical parts. We need also to remind ourselves that conclusions about the importance of instructional leadership are not completely uniform and are consistently richer and more robust in qualitative than in quantitative studies. As we will see momentarily, research that includes both direct and indirect impacts are always more sanguine about the effects of leadership than those that include only direct effects. In addition, the significance of context is ignored at peril. We also must acknowledge that the job is larger than leadership for school improvement. We close with one last caution. The work of principals is difficult by nature. It is much easier to write about the leadership game than it is to practice leadership.

The framework for our work is contained in Figure 4.1. In order to push toward "the elusive goal of clarifying the link between leadership and learning" (Wahlstrom & Louis, 2008, p. 459), we partition the narrative into segments. We open with a description of the antecedents that exercise purchase on school improvement leadership. We include here demographic conditions, knowledge and skills, values and beliefs, and traits and characteristics. Next, we explore school contextual variables that shape leadership practice. We then turn to leadership behaviors inside the

Figure 4.1   Leadership for School Improvement

Academic Press and Culture of Support

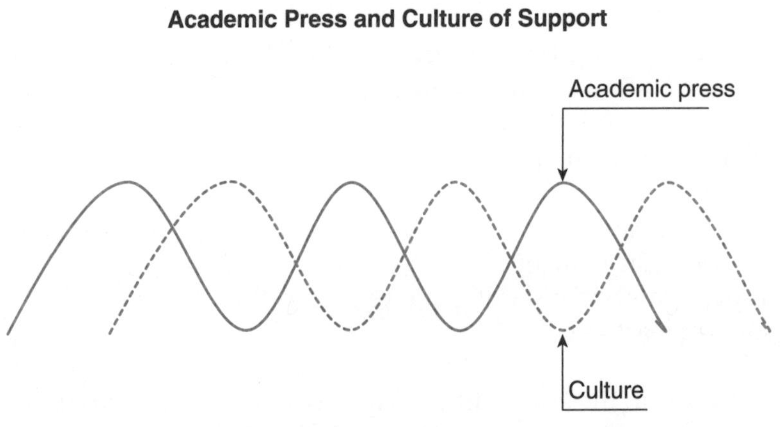

domains of effective schools. Here, we foreground material on leading the instructional program that is the focus of the remaining chapters of the book. An analysis of the pathways of leader influence on the workings of the school closes our discussion of the framework.

To complete our assignment, it is necessary to compartmentalize findings. To some extent, this is artificial. School improvement is complex and messy. It is difficult at times to slice it into components. Ideas and findings crisscross the narrative and are interwoven across sections of the story. What is true for school improvement holds for leadership for school improvement as well. Additionally, the work we present represents the normal pathway to success. However, we must remember that there is no universal chronicle that is applicable at all times and in all situations. Also, for reasons detailed earlier, our attention in the model is devoted almost exclusively to variables linked to student learning. That is, ours is a constrained model. This focus is not intended to gainsay the importance of other elements of school leadership. Recall also that ours is a hinged or reciprocal model. That is, the principal both is directed by antecedents, environmental and school contexts, and school conditions and outcomes and influences these factors. The model is multilevel and dynamic, not static—a fact that can be forgotten when it is pulled apart for analysis.

ANTECEDENTS

The most sophisticated and theoretically sound models of instructional leadership include a set of personal factors that shape the actions of principals and, in turn, are molded by those actions. While there is overlap within and across antecedent categories, they do provide a useful heuristic for understanding how personal conditions shape school improvement leadership. Building on our earlier work in this area, we propose four broad bundles of antecedents: demographic characteristics, knowledge and skills, values and beliefs, and traits.

The demographic antecedents of leadership behavior include gender, age, education, and experience. Research confirms connections for gender, especially for instructionally centered actions, education, and prior teaching experience. Linkages between age or stage of development and administrative experience have yet to be established.

In terms of knowledge and skills, there is research evidence that the intellectual or cognitive capacities of principals have sway on behavior, which in turn impacts school effectiveness. "General and domain specific expertise" (Zaccaro, Kemp, & Bader, 2004, p. 120) are influential as well. Relatedly, social-emotional capacities of principals shape actions and sequela to those behaviors. Important elements here include tolerance for ambiguity; self-awareness, especially of one's emotions; self-efficacy; interpersonal skills such as empathy and social appraisal skills;

and coping skills. There is also some suggestion that intellectual acumen and social-emotional intelligence together exercise powerful effects on the behavior of leaders.

While there is more overlap here than was the case with the demographic and knowledge antecedents, linkages between values and beliefs (and dispositions) are also more robust. To begin, there is a sizable body of evidence that "values and beliefs inform the principal's decisions and actions" (Silins & Mulford, 2010, p. 74) and impact school success. While it is foolhardy to attempt to compile a complete list of all the values that mold leader behavior, some dispositions rise to the level of high visibility and importance. That is, there are value-behavior linkages that influence school improvement. One is a ferocious belief in the educability of children and the prime mission of ensuring their success. A second is a disposition toward equity and justice. A third is the belief in the power of the community of stakeholders to arrive at decisions that are best for students, a disposition toward collaboration.

Research on traits and their linkages to leader behavior and subsequent organizational performance has enjoyed a checkered history. Originally, they held center stage in explanations of leader effects. They were then pushed off the stage altogether only to claw their way partially back into the spotlight in the last few years. Traits are best thought of "as relatively stable and coherent integrations of personal characteristics that foster a consistent pattern of leadership performance across a variety of group and organizational situations" (Zaccaro et al., 2004. p. 104). The most accurate conclusion we can draw is that traits do mold behavior. The fact that other antecedents and context variables also matter hardly diminishes the "personological" basis of leadership (Judge, Bono, Ilies, & Gerhardt, 2002, p. 775). As was the case with beliefs, containers for characteristics can seem bottomless. They do cohere, however, into a handful of "common and consistent" elements (Gurr, Drysdale, & Mulford, 2005, p. 548): passion, optimism, persistence, authenticity, and a penchant for hard work (high energy).

Passion means that principals are proactive. They have a bias toward action, risk-taking, and innovation. A results orientation is also part of proactiveness, as is a personal dedication to obtaining those ends and a penchant for inspiring others to do likewise. Passion includes courage, especially to make difficult and unpopular decisions. Passionate leaders are comfortable pushing back the boundaries that limit goal achievement.

Faith and optimism often move leaders to action. This includes a predilection for positive thinking, especially in times of uncertainty. Leader optimism produces behaviors that help others gain and maintain positive perspectives. Optimistic leaders help people see the connections between their work and the success of students; they spread a sense of possibility.

Successful school leaders are often quite persistent. They translate that sense of tenacity into actions that push, pull, and carry their colleagues to higher levels of effectiveness. They are "determined individuals" in the pursuit of goals (Southworth, 2002, p. 82).

Strong leaders are often defined as authentic, a characteristic that covers a good deal of ground. It includes what researchers describe as *openness to others*. Embedded here also are feelings of empathy and concern for others as well as a sense of conscientiousness, which includes dependability and consideration. Authenticity suggests a stance of non-guardedness and trustworthiness. Gurr and others (2006, p. 375) refer to it as "other centeredness," commitments to inclusiveness, honesty, and accessibility.

Many productive leaders are high-energy people with powerful work ethics, what Southworth (2002) describes as "an emblem that the leader is devoted to the school" (p. 82). This energy fuels actions that promote organizational health and student learning.

THE SCHOOL IMPROVEMENT LEADERSHIP ENGINE

In the remainder of the book, we explore the instructional dimension of the model in Figure 4.1, what we think of as half of the engine of school improvement leadership. Our objective here is simply to provide an overview of forthcoming analyses. As we will see, paradoxically, our engine is surprisingly simple yet complex. Each element carries depth and nuance that belie simple labels. Most of the concepts are not mutually exclusive; there is a fair amount of overlap between and among them. Variables wrap around each other and mix together. At times, ingredients fall under the spotlight. At other times, they are backstage. Varied proportions and different weights hold at different times and places. Variables can be combined in various ways to fuel school improvement. The relationships among the pieces are complex. There is no single storyline. What we end up with looks a good deal like a stew or is, in many ways, similar to disentangling thickets. While this labor is essential, it is messy and, at times, less satisfactory than we might wish.

Tasks

My colleague Philip Hallinger and I have held for the past 30 years that leadership needs to be defined, eventually, in terms of observable and consequential practices. For us then, school improvement leadership is the enactment of behaviorally anchored processes in the core dimensions of improving and effective schools (e.g., monitoring instruction, building linkages with parents, establishing growth targets for students). It is always a cocktail of functions and processes, of content and ways.

Since the inception of the effective schools movement in the late 1970s and early 1980s, analysts have provided a multitude of frameworks to capture school improvement leadership. In one of the earliest, based on their California study of effective schools, Murphy and Hallinger (1989) featured the following domains (framing school goals and objectives, developing and promoting expectations, developing and promoting standards, assessing and monitoring student performance, protecting instructional time, knowledge of curriculum and instruction, promoting curricular coordination, promoting and supporting instructional improvement, supervision and evaluation of instruction, and creating productive work environment) and processes (communication, conflict resolution, group processes, decision making, and change processes). Around the same time, Sweeney (1982) culled out six core bundles of actions that define school improvement leadership: highlight student achievement, establish common instructional strategies, foster a safe and orderly environment, monitor student progress, coordinate the instructional program, and nurture and support teachers.

Leithwood, alone and with a variety of colleagues, has been extremely influential in crafting broad frameworks of leadership for school improvement. Perhaps his best known model features setting direction, developing people, redesigning the organization, and managing the instructional program (Leithwood, Patten, & Jantzi, 2010). Another framework includes goals, culture, participatory decision making, and connections to parents and communities, along with the practices to bring these ingredients to life in schools (Leithwood, Seashore Louis, Anderson, & Wahlstrom, 2004).

Other scholars highlight the role of the principal as developer of capital in their portraits of leadership (Fullan & Ballew, 2002). Spillane, Diamond, Walker, Halverson, and Jita (2001) focus on human, social, and physical capital. Smerdon and Borman (2009) underscore human, material, and social capital. From our analyses of capital perspectives, we suggest that leadership for school improvement is best understood in terms of six types of capital: human, production, resource, cultural, social, and integrative.

Other designs have been employed as well. For example, May and Supovitz (2011) partition school improvement leadership into practices, styles, and processes. In her review, Cotton (2003) outlines overarching domains of principal work (with embedded practices): a clear focus on student learning interactions and relationships, culture, instruction, and accountability. Bryk and colleagues (2010) define leadership anchored to school improvement as the ability to positively impact instructional guidance, professional capacity, school community connections, and a student-focused environment.

In one model, Hallinger and Heck (1998) unpack leadership behaviors into four essential domains: purpose and goals, organizational structure and social networks, people, and organizational culture. In another (Hallinger & Heck, 1996), they describe five roles: being a catalyst for change, maintaining an improvement focus, fostering the leadership of others, supporting instructional effectiveness, and providing tangible support for youngsters and teachers. Supovitz, Sirinides, and May (2010) wrestle behaviors into three pens: focusing mission and goals, encouraging a climate of collaboration and trust, and supporting instructional improvement. Fullan (2002, p. 2) outlines five "action-and-mind-sets": moral purpose, dynamics of change, emotional intelligence, coherence making, and knowledge.

In our work, we build from these and other empirically anchored frameworks about school improvement leadership over the last 35 years. We employ two domains to capture the essence of school improvement leadership, managing the instructional program and creating productive culture. The processes are threaded into those dimensions—visible but not always in the spotlight. For this reason, it is useful to say a few words about the processes before we proceed. One can identify a great assortment of processes (e.g., communicating) that give meaning to content (e.g., instruction) from the research on leadership for school improvement. Many of these come from studies of leadership and the various lines of analysis on school improvement (e.g., school restructuring, turnaround schools, comprehensive school reform, achievement-gap-closing schools). Others are found buried in studies addressing a plethora of other areas of interest (e.g., professional development, programs for English language learners or homeless children). We group many of these processes into three bundles: organizational functioning processes, human relations processes, and inspirational processes. Organizational functioning processes include planning, organizing, implementing, coordinating, resourcing, monitoring, boundary spanning and buffering, and assessing. Human relations processes feature problem framing and problem solving, decision making, communication, and conflict resolution. Inspirational processes include modeling, teaching, maintaining visibility, and sense making.

Before leaving our overview of tasks (the cocktail of content and processes), it is important to introduce what we refer to as the *characteristic elements of leadership practices*. To begin with, there is the issue of the *quality* of practices, which can be arrayed on a continuum from effective to poor. Practices also vary in *frequency*, from routinely performed to rarely undertaken. *Scope*, a characteristic first empirically surfaced by May and Supovitz (2011), addresses the number (or percentage) of people touched by a leader's practice, from one to all. *Intensity* is an important element of practice as well, ranging from high or deep to light. *Range* addresses the coverage of behaviors from few to many. *Integration* refers to the extent to which practices are discrete or tightly bundled.

Over the last half century, a good deal of ink has been devoted to the topic of leadership style, "the modes by which principals express themselves" (May & Supovitz, 2011, p. 335). Early analyses focused on whether principals were task-oriented or people-oriented. Derivations of this work often define style in terms of directiveness, supportiveness, and formality.

Another line of work considers style in terms of power and control. One strand here focuses on whether the principal displays an authoritarian or democratic style of leadership. A second addresses style in terms of whether the principal holds power centrally or distributes it to staff. A third genre of work presents style in terms of the leader's penchant for professional or hierarchical control.

Bolman and Deal (2008) help us see the ways principals express themselves somewhat differently, defining style by the frames that leaders employ—political, structural, symbolic, and human. Still others define style in terms of leader activeness, from highly active to laissez-faire. Building on the work of Burns (1978) and other seminal scholars in the area of organizational leadership, Leithwood and Jantzi (2000, 2005, 2006) introduced the topic of transactional and transformational leadership styles to education. Closely related here are the discussions of charismatic versus noncharismatic styles.

Styles anchored in the nature of work privileged by the leader has been common, at least since the pioneering efforts of Cuban (1988), who highlights political, managerial, and instructional orientations. Style has also been presented in terms of whether the leader features authority-based, morally based, or personality-based practices. We see a good deal of writing featuring change in analyses of style as well, with principals being characterized as either status-quo leaders or change-oriented leaders (proactive, innovative, risk-taking individuals). Finally, the idea of integrative styles has arisen over time.

The collective body of scholarship on leadership style has been helpful in mapping important dimensions of school improvement leadership work, deepening the leadership narrative. On the other hand, evidence on the effectiveness of styles has been both elusive and largely noncumulative. Looking at the full array of work, here is what we can report with some degree of confidence. There is no one best style for all places and times. Leaders with varying orientations have been identified as effective. Alignment between leader style and context seems worthy of further investigation. There is some sense that leaders of improving schools are often authoritative (not *authoritarian*) and that a laissez-faire or passive leadership style is rarely productive and often proves to be quite problematic. Styles that highlight distributed or shared leadership have yet to be linked tightly with improvement, while those that feature commitment to learning and teaching often are found to characterize principals in improving schools.

Leadership Pathways

Earlier, we reported that principals' effects on students are largely indirect. Their actions are mediated by the instructional program and the school culture (see Figure 4.1). Here, we add that principal effects on these mediating variables can be direct or indirect as well. For example, a principal can visit a classroom and provide feedback to an individual teacher. Or she can meet with a grade-level team to think through some curricular issues.

These are direct effects on teachers. Alternatively, principals can do things that in turn touch teachers or shape school climate. For example, a principal can create time to permit and protocols to guide collaborative work. Or he can require the use of curricular pacing guides. These actions have indirect effects on teachers. Something is situated between the principal and the teacher.

Researchers have also uncovered the mechanisms by which principals operationalize indirect effects on teachers and culture. School structures (e.g., how the day is organized, where teachers are located in the building) provide one influence strategy. Policies provide a second (e.g., all teachers cover both high- and low-track classes, all special education students must be mainstreamed). Standard operating procedures and norms (ingrained routines, systems, and expectations) offer principals a third indirect avenue of influence (e.g., staff members personally greet each child at the classroom door every class period). Tools and artifacts provide another avenue of impacting teachers and culture indirectly (e.g., meeting protocols, lesson plan formats). Finally, principals exercise indirect leadership by the way they allocate resources. Leadership activity across all five of these pathways shapes the ways teachers conduct their work.

We underscore both direct and indirect pathways in our analyses of creating instructional capacity in Chapters 5 through 8. Both appear to be influential in the process of school improvement, although the use of direct approaches is often constrained by factors such as school size and level (i.e., elementary vs. secondary).

CONCLUSION

In this chapter, we presented the model undergirding our work on leadership for school improvement. We unpacked the essential personal factors (antecedents) that help shape leader practice. We also described factors in the school's environment (context) that push and pull leaders to act in certain ways. We closed with a preliminary look at the school improvement leadership engine, the tasks (the processes linked to domains) that define effective leadership, and the pathways (direct and indirect) that practices follow. At the foundational level, we reported that effective school leadership is defined by creating productive cultures and managing the instructional program. In the remainder of the book, we turn to specifics about molding a high-quality instructional program.

PART III

Building Instructional Capacity

5

Staffing, Time and Material Resources, and Support

In Part III, we report that teachers are the essential resources in schools. Here, we deepen that position by concluding that since "organizations depend on the quality of their people" (Bryk, Sebring, Allensworth, Luppescu, & Easton, 2010, p. 54), instructional capacity is the most significant theme in the school improvement narrative. Researchers and developers often refer to issues such as capital and talent management. Inside the education profession, it is best to link this concept more concretely to our own work, to employ the idea of instructional capital or capacity, or, stated more directly, "a primary channel through which principals can be expected to improve the quality of teachers is through teacher transitions that improve the caliber of the workforce" (Branch, Rivkin, & Hanushek, 2003, p. 5).

In Chapters 5 and 6, we look at professional capacity in considerable detail. We partition the concept into four parts: staffing, time and material resources, and support in Chapter 5 and talent development in Chapter 6. Before we do so, however, we provide some important contextual comments. First, what Bryk and colleagues (2010, p. 54) refer to as the "human resources subsystem" is especially critical in high-human, low-technology-based industries. Remember here that over 80 percent of each school dollar is devoted to people. Second, instructional capacity is particularly important in schools with large numbers of students in peril. It is also more difficult to grow in these schools. Third, and relatedly, capacity building is extremely important for schools in difficult circumstances. Fourth, principals are a key lever in fostering instructional capacity, or as Branch and associates (2003) capture it, "the management of teacher quality is an important pathway through which principals affect school quality" (p. 5).

STAFFING

To begin with, there is abundant evidence that "the collective capacity of a school-based professional community is contingent on the quality of the staff recruited into the school" (Bryk et al., 2010, p. 57) and that "recruiting capable teachers is critical to the breadth and depth of expertise needed to undertake school improvement" (pp. 54–55; see also Table. 5.1.) That is, "[I]t is difficult to produce positive discernments of competence and integrity when teachers are not competent" (Kochanek, 2005, p. 21).

What is true for teacher recruitment is true for teacher selection as well. Indeed, research informs us that "the teacher selection process [has] a sizeable, statistically significant effect on student achievement gains" (Brewer, 1993, p. 282). And again, across 35 years of research, we find that effective principals are personally and deeply involved with well-thought-out teacher selection processes.

Research helps us see that capacity building extends beyond recruitment and selection. For example, it shows us that capacity building addresses retention and that leadership, as it was in previous functions, is a critical element here (Sather, 1999). Capacity building also captures the allocation or assignment of teacher talent. As York-Barr and Duke (2004, p. 290) inform us, at one level, this occurs through the thoughtful matching of "the unique and varied leadership capacities of individual teachers with the unique and varied leadership functions" in the school. Careful attention to mentoring assignments is important here, as are additional training opportunities for teachers assigned to help people schoolwide with functions such as managing data or facilitating technology use or roles such as instructional coaches (Goldstein, 2004; Wohlstetter, Datnow, & Park, 2008; Youngs, 2007). The assignment of teachers to important cross-class responsibilities is also significant. We describe all this as the allocation of teachers to other teachers and to schoolwide improvement work (Murphy, 2005; Timperley, 2009).

At a second level, allocation occurs as leaders move teachers to "assignments that result in a better fit between the needs of the students and the talents of teachers" (Leithwood & Montgomery, 1982, p. 325). Important here is the assignment of teachers to subjects and grade levels for which they are formally prepared and in which they are certified (Cosner, 2011). The major conclusion on this second dimension of allocation is that "the careful assignment of teachers to classes is unquestionably a critical leadership function" (Blase & Kirby, 2009, p. 68) because "at the classroom level, effective leaders are directly involved in matching teachers with students" (Leithwood & Montgomery, 1982, p. 334). This leadership assignment function takes on added significance for students placed at risk (Oakes & Guiton, 1995; Quint, 2006).

There is a growing body of evidence that effective leaders bolster instructional capacity by moving less-than-successful, inadequate, and uncaring teachers from their schools, either through transfer or termination (Finnigan & Gross, 2007). They understand that "high performing teams do not carry C [level] players for long" (Tichy & Cardwell, 2004, p. 9) and that "incompetent teachers not only harm the children in their classrooms, but they also call into question the dedication and competence of the entire staff" (Kochanek, 2005, p. 91). Transfer is used as a capacity-building tool in two ways by school leaders. To begin with, leaders counsel teachers to move to positions that provide a better fit for their skills and/or values and points of view about teaching and learning. They also exert pressure so that teachers understand that it is in their best interest to teach elsewhere or, perhaps, seek out different lines of work or retire (Cotton, 2003; Goldstein, 2004). Effective leaders are also less reluctant than their peers to terminate teachers' employment in their schools (Johnson & Asera, 1999; Spillane, Diamond, Walker, Halverson, & Jita, 2001).

Capacity building is enhanced when leaders are aggressive in not accepting weak teachers and teachers who do not fit with the school's vision and values. They push back against requests from the district that would undermine school cohesion and student learning.

Finally, instructional capacity is about leaders carrying out efforts to insure that effective teachers stay at their schools. We know in general that teachers remain at their schools because they have effective principals. In addition, effective principals use a plethora of strategies to hold on to good teachers. We present some of these below.

It is one thing to report that instructional capacity is critical in improving outcomes for children and that principals are essential in making the human capital aspects of the system function well. But the question of what the criteria for this work should be requires probing. We know that principals need to make staffing a priority. Principals model what is important by how they spend their time more so than by what they say. So, to begin with, considerable time needs to be allotted to the staffing functions and greater "regard for the human resources necessary to make the system actually work" (Bryk et al., 2010, p. 206) is required. Second, principals need to carve out as much autonomy and influence over staffing functions as possible. They cannot allow bureaucratic and political considerations to hold the high ground. Rather, they need to be powerful advocates for their schools and their students. If there is one venue where it is wise to be the squeaky wheel, this is it.

Diving deeper, principals need to look carefully at criteria that make a difference while pushing aside those that are less influential. And all the while, they must hold firm to the knowledge (1) that there is no single criteria that can carry the day and (2) that a collection of smaller forces can bring large impacts. Let us start with an examination of what is often minimized in staffing positions. We know that a number of the key indicators historically employed here are not particularly robust. Included here are educational degrees, coursework, grades earned, teacher evaluations, and certification in general (Borman & Kimball, 2005; Hattie, 2009; Nye, Konstantopoulos, & Hedges, 2004; Wayne & Youngs, 2003). Attention to less-visible and rarely used background factors makes more empirical sense. Here, scholars highlight (1) ratings of the universities from which candidates graduate; (2) intellectual ability or scores on standardized measures of achievement, especially verbal ability (Thompson & O'Quinn, 2001; Wayne & Youngs, 2003); and (3) subject matter knowledge (Hattie, 2009; Hill, Rowan, & Ball, 2005). In the world of instructional capacity, these are stronger measures than the ones we have relied on for so long (Flanagan & Grissmer, 2002; Grissmer, Flanagan, & Williamson, 1998).

Moving beyond background characteristics, research confirms the hallmark place in terms of student learning of a number of "softer" elements that teachers do (or do not) bring to the job. Passion for the work in general and a deep sense of caring for children and young persons are critically important, as is the ability to turn that passion and caring into trusting relationships (Johnson & Asera, 1999; Murphy & Torre, 2014). There is also considerable evidence that the care and specificity with which schools define their values and vision and the ability of leaders to use staffing to align human resources with those missions is related to more pronounced student learning (Desimone, 2002; Huberman, Parrish, Hannan, Arellanes, & Shambaugh, 2011). Attention to staffing in regard to fluency with culturally appropriate pedagogy seems important (Auerbach, 2007).

TIME AND MATERIAL RESOURCES

Time

Principals impact instructional capacity by how they value and address the essential resource of time, "a potent variable affecting student learning" (Firestone & Wilson, 1985, p. 12). Effective leaders have a sixth sense for the importance of this scarce resource (Blase & Kirby, 2009). They understand "that it is a finite and valuable resource that is sometimes squandered by competing demands and conflicting priorities" (Leithwood, Seashore Louis, Anderson, & Wahlstrom, 2004, p. 57). For example, when

Table 5.1   Building Instructional Capacity

Staffing	Time	Support
Recruitment	Extend	Emotional
Selection	Allocate	Appraisal Organizational Systems
Assigning	Protect	
Removing	Use	
Retaining		

one computes the academic learning time (academic content and rate of engagement and of success), the big number of 420 minutes per day drops dramatically. Principals who see "real" time in schools in this manner understand that it is a resource that needs to be safeguarded (Creemers & Reezigt, 1996; Yair, 2000).

Effective school leaders also insure that the significant variability in the use of time in schools is compressed (Bryk et al., 2010). They allocate their own time in ways that enhance the quality of teaching and learning in the school (Johnson & Asera, 1999). As is the case with other resources such as funding, because "daily, weekly, and annual schedules have a substantial impact on the time available for instruction" (Firestone & Wilson, 1985 p. 12), effective leaders are proactive in their efforts to add to the available time in the school (Cotton, 2003). Strategies here include lengthening the school day, week, and/or year, either for all children or for those who are the most in need of extra assistance (Conchas, 2001; Johnson & Asera, 1999; Murphy, 2010).

Effective leaders are also good at adding time within the school day for subject areas deemed most essential for student success, generally English (reading) and mathematics (Balfanz, Herzog, & MacIver, 2007). Again, we see that this strategy can apply to all children or to the children with the greatest needs (Auerbach, 2009; Betts, Zau, & Koedel, 2010). Equally important, effective leaders are attentive to how time is allocated within the school day. Most importantly, "they allocate more time to tasks directly related to the teaching-learning process" (Goldring & Pasternack, 1994, p. 241) and work to insure that time is devoted to engagement with challenging academic materials (Hattie, 2009; Yair, 2000).

On a third front, leaders in effective schools are diligent in protecting overall allotment of available time. As noted above, they work with tenacity to ensure that time is not squandered. Researchers have uncovered a number of general and specific strategies in play here. On one hand, these leaders buffer teachers from "intrusive forces" (Dannetta, 2002, p. 162) that usurp time: "They give teachers time to teach" (Blase & Kirby, 2009, p. 73). They protect teaching time from district and school management and from community actions that negatively impact learning time. They also protect time by establishing a safe and supportive culture that minimizes student disruptions (Leithwood, Anderson, Mascall, & Strauss, 2011; Robinson, Lloyd, & Rowe, 2008).

Finally, effective leaders are proactive in shaping the use of time in classrooms (Hallinger & Murphy, 1985; Murphy, 1990b). They forge consistent schoolwide understandings about time use (Creemers & Reezigt, 1996). They cooperate with and support teachers to ensure that classes begin and end on time and that minimal amounts of time are lost due to transitions during class periods (O'Donnell & White, 2005; Scanlan & Lopez, 2012). Since the average student is actively participating in class only about half the time, principals are diligent in helping teachers use strategies to enhance engagement (Murphy & Torre, 2014). They work to insure that teachers present students with meaningful and challenging material and authentic assessments—"active and energizing pedagogies" (Balfanz et al., 2007, p. 231)—not continuous teacher talk (Goodlad, 1984; Hattie, 2009).

Material Resources

To this point in Chapter 5, we have examined staffing and time. Here, we focus on material resources. As was the case with staffing and time, we know that leaders' attention to materials is important for the implementation and improvement of instruction and student learning (Desimone, 2002; Spillane et al., 2001). There is extensive evidence that effective leaders are proactive in identifying material resources to strengthen their schools and classroom instruction in particular (Blase & Blase, 2004; Cotton, 2003; Eilers & Camacho, 2007). They turn up more community, grant-based, and district resources, oftentimes because they have invested the time to develop positive and trusting relationships with the actors in these three sectors (Beachum & Dentith, 2004; Eilers & Camacho, 2007). Equally important, effective leaders understand that it is not about securing resources *per se* but rather about securing resources that are linked to school goals (Robinson et al., 2008). Material resources sought and garnered include instructional material such as books, tools, equipment, technology, and supplies (Clark, Dyson, Millward, & Robson, 1999; Supovitz & Christman, 2003).

Again, as was the case with time, the role of the leader is only half completed with the identification and securing of additional resources. Equally important is the fact that effective school leaders are adept at the employment of material resources (Sweeney, 1982). Here, we learn that because "the possession of resources does not automatically translate into their use in efforts to lead change in instruction" (Spillane et al., 2001, p. 927); that is, it is the use or activation of material resources that is most important (Sweeney, 1982). Spillane and his team (2001, p. 937) note that "the skills with which these resources are configured by school leaders" is the central issue.

We see here that effective leaders ensure that materials are used in the intended manner, including customization to the local context (Newmann, Smith, Allensworth, & Bryk, 2001; Supovitz & Christman, 2003). "Creative configuration and activation of resources is critical" (Spillane et al., 2001, p. 921). Robinson (2007) refers to this as the *strategic dimension* of resource allocation. The critical issue is the ability of leaders to integrate material resources "with regard for the coherence and strategic alignment of resulting activities" (p. 13), what Malen and Rice (2004, p. 636) describe as "the degree of correspondence between resources that are available and the resources that are required to accomplish organizational goals."

SUPPORT

Here, we continue our discussion of how leaders can help build instructional capacity in their schools. The spotlight is on support for teachers in addition to materials and time treated above. The perhaps obvious but still needed point is that principal support is a cardinal element in the equation of leadership effectiveness (Cotton, 2003). Indeed, teachers often inform us that it is the hallmark element (Leithwood, Patten, & Jantzi, 2010).

A few notes are helpful before we unpack the concept of leader support for teachers. We know from research studies and the wisdom of practice that it is a difficult construct to corral. Or, as Mangin notes (2007, p. 326), the "notion of support is inherently elusive owing to its subjective manner." And as Littrell and associates (1994) extend this point, "[D]efining support is a multidimensional concept that includes a wide range of behaviors" (p. 297). Metaphorically, support is more akin to a stew than it is a dish of distinct foods (Murphy, Beck, Crawford, & Hodges, 2001).

It is also helpful to expose some of the embedded concepts in the narrative around support, insights that are easy to lose sight of in the rush of leaders' frenetic work schedules. We know, for example, that not all support work is equal. Supports can be categorized across the continuum from low-level to high-level activities (May & Supovitz, 2011). Researchers and practitioners also remind us that support is often informal as well as formal in design (Leithwood, Jantzi, & Steinbach, 1999; Penuel et al., 2010). Supovitz and Poglinco (2001), in turn, reinforce one of the essential conclusions here. That is, context is always critical. In this case, they confirm that support is "dependent on the personality and temperament of the principal, the particular needs of individual teachers, and the environment of the school" (p. 16).

The literature helps us see that support is bifurcated. At times, the focus is on subtraction—taking away problems, reducing ambiguities, buffering unhelpful forces, and removing organizational barriers. At other times, the focus is on additions—augmenting actions. As with most issues in schools, there is a difference between assessments of the amount of support teachers desire and the amount of support they see coming their way from principals (Littrell et al., 1994).

Researchers, developers, and practitioners have developed a variety of frames to array support. Crum and Sherman (2008) define *principal support* as understanding, encouraging, and empowering teachers. Leithwood and colleagues (1999) employ the concept as individualized support, a construct that stands above others in the platform of transformational leadership practices. Supovitz and Poglinco (2001) suggest that principals' support for teachers materializes through the provision of resources, counseling, and encouragement. Gurr and team (2005, p. 4) find that leaders provide three types of support: one-off or cross-crisis support, support for individuals as they undergo change processes, and ongoing support in the form of acknowledging others. Finally, House (cited in Littrell et al., 1994) created a four-dimensional framework to describe support: emotional support, instrumental support, informational support, and appraisal support. Building on these different formulations, we examine support below in three main categories: emotional support, appraisal support, and organizational systems support. Before we do so, however, we make explicit the power of the support tool for school leaders.

Support has been shown to have powerful, positive effects across an array of organizational conditions and outcomes, including the following:

- augmentation of teacher leadership (York-Barr & Duke, 2004)
- positive sense of self for teachers (Littrell et al., 1994)
- teacher commitment to school goals (Riehl & Sipple, 1996)
- teacher personal health (Littrell et al., 1994)
- quality and range of instruction (Blase & Blase, 2004; Mangin, 2007)
- implementation of change efforts (Datnow & Castellano, 2001; Louis & Miles, 1990)
- increased emphasis on student achievement (Sweeney, 1982)
- enhancement of teacher trust (Youngs, 2007)
- school culture and climate (Supovitz, Sirinides, & May, 2010)
- teacher morale (Leithwood et al., 1999)
- student learning outcomes (Hoy, Hannum, & Tschannen-Moran,1998; Mulford & Silins, 2003)
- overall school performance (Heck, 2000; Robinson, 2007)

Emotional Support

Emotional support is at the heart of capacity-building work. Analysts describe emotional support in a variety of ways and with varying tones. The overarching idea that gives meaning to the subdimensions of support is trust or, more specifically, caring and trusting relationships between the principal and the teacher (Murphy & Torre, 2014; Youngs, 2007). Scholars reveal that trust can be described in a number of overlapping ways, including through assorted behaviors that "communicate the leader's respect for his or her colleagues and concerns about their personal feelings and needs" (Leithwood, 2006, p. 31) and "being open, supportive, and friendly" (Leithwood et al., 2011, p. 16). It includes actions that convey an openness to new ideas and the freedom to learn from mistakes as well as the sense that the leader is clearly part of the team (Blase & Blase, 2000; Supovitz & Poglinco, 2001). It encompasses efforts to recognize accomplishments (Chavis, Ward, Elwell, & Barret, 1997).

Nurturing is an essential aspect of trusting relations (Blase & Kirby, 2009). It includes elements such as going to bat for teachers or giving moral support, showing concern, being considerate, and showing sensitivity (Barnett, McCormick, & Conners, 2001; Chavis et al., 1997; Leithwood et al., 1999; Mayrowetz & Weinstein, 1999; Walker & Slear, 2011). Listening to the personal needs of teachers and treating each teacher uniquely are often discussed in the literature on emotional support (Leithwood, 2011; May & Supovitz, 2011). Affording respect is part of the narrative. So, too, are providing voice and hearing opinions (Hayes, Christie, Mills, & Lingard, 2004). Using an inquiry approach to working with staff is supportive (Blase & Blase, 2004). Undergirding nurturing are the principles of fairness in dealing with staff, asset-based understandings of teacher colleagues, and personal approachability (Kochanek, 2005; Lomotey, 1989; Wohlstetter et al., 2008).

We learn from an assortment of investigations that principal interpersonal leadership skills are essential in fostering nurturing relationships. Communication skills are particularly important, especially authentic hearing (Beachum & Dentith, 2004; Walker & Slear, 2011). The ability to resolve conflicts rather than allowing them to undermine relationships is also highlighted in the research (Robinson, 2008).

There is a thick line of research over the past 40 years on the importance of principal involvement, attentiveness, and visibility in promoting nurturing relationships (Johnson & Asera, 1999; Murphy & Torre, 2014). Supportive principals are approachable (Kochanek, 2005). They interact in both formal and informal ways with staff (Youngs, 2007). In the process, they foster trust and grow a "more productive and stimulating environment" (Littrell, 1994, p. 306).

Embedded in our analysis is the fact that in the domain of emotional support, "the most powerful example is the principal herself or himself" (Blase & Kirby, 2009, p. 27). Thus we find role modeling at the heart of emotional support (Crum & Sherman, 2008), "providing appropriate models of best practice and beliefs considered fundamental to the organization" (Littrell et al., 1994, p. 9). Indeed, in effective schools staff report that principals are "sources of advice about teaching problems" (Robinson, 2008, p. 667). In these schools, "teachers discern an ability and willingness on the principal's part to model appropriate behavior" (Blase & Kirby, 2009, p. 29). Such modeling leads to improvements in teacher's thinking, instruction in classrooms, and school culture (May & Supovitz, 2011). The opposite is true as well. When principals are "absent from the daily life of the school" (Youngs, 2007, p. 122) and this modeling is absent, teachers often struggle (Cooper, 1996). Modeling in the literature includes discussing instructional expectations, developing and using protocols, demonstrating teaching techniques with and for teachers, making suggestions, being personally involved in problem solving and implementation work, sharing one's own personal experiences, and encouraging teacher leadership (Blanc et al., 2010; Blase & Blase, 2004; Johnson & Asera, 1999; Louis & Miles, 1990; Walker & Slear, 2011).

In a similar vein, emotional support occurs when principals act as facilitators and counselors for teachers (Bryk et al., 2010). As Robinson, Lloyd, and Rowe (2008, p. 663) discovered, principals are "significantly more likely to be nominated as sources of advice in higher achieving schools." The involvement and accessibility discussed earlier, in turn, provides avenues for principals to shape teaching activity (Mangin, 2007). A "key dimension of this advisory role is an accessible, nonintrusive attentiveness to teachers' concerns" (Friedkin & Slater, 1994, p. 150).

Appraisal Support

In their study, Littrell and associates (1994) found that appraisal support was second to emotional support in importance. For purposes of analysis, we partition appraisal support into two dimensions, acknowledging that they are two intertwined elements rather than discrete categories: feedback and praise/recognition. As we report below, each is highly valued by teachers, associated with effective school leaders, and linked to important organizational outcomes. In his cardinal analysis, Hattie (2009, p. 12) lays out the significance of the first aspect of our chronicle here when he reports "that the most powerful single influence on achievement is feedback, . . . that the most important feature [is] the creation of situations in classrooms for the teachers to receive more feedback about their teaching." It is clear then that leaders must be aggressive in this area, including making themselves accessible to discuss classroom-based work.

While this is not the place to lay out all of the qualities of positive feedback in general, those characteristics that find a home in the appraisal system do merit some attention. We learn from the research, for example, that feedback addressed in a collaborative stance or that offers "mutual engagement" (Coldren & Spillane, 2007, p. 376) is desirable (Blase & Blase, 2004). "Thoughtful discourse" (Blase & Blase, 2000, p. 133) is important as well, a time for explanation and back-and-forth discussion among participants (Blase & Blase, 2004). It is critically important that the principal be viewed as knowledgeable and credible (Leithwood et al., 1999). Blase and Blase (2004, p. 22) provide specificity to this characteristic when they describe *credibility* as "knowledge and mastery of a number of complex prerequisite skills and processes." Appraisal feedback should be specific and anchored in care and individual consideration (Blase & Blase, 2000). It should be provided in a nonthreatening manner (Hayes et al., 2004). It should provide salient and actionable information as well as information about teachers' efforts to enhance student learning (Robinson, 2007). Thus, appraisal feedback should be "detailed and descriptive" (Blase & Blase, 2004, p. 39) and provide teachers "with alternative suggestions to what they [are] doing" (p. 135). Robinson (2007, p. 15) concludes that not all feedback is equal: "[F]eedback about learning processes may be more effective than feedback about outcomes and feedback that is linked to a corrective strategy is more helpful than one that is not."

Absent or infrequent feedback is unhelpful. So, too, is punitive feedback and feedback that threatens the self-esteem of teachers (Blase & Blase, 2004). Feedback that fails to promote self-reflection is also of limited value. For example, in the Blase and Blase (2004, p. 46) study, "[T]eachers explained that ineffective principals who did post observation conferences frequently failed to provide any growth-promoting constructive feedback about their observations." Such activity causes teacher to lose "respect and trust in their principals, causes a drop in teacher motivation and self-esteem, [and] increases anger and sense of futility" (p. 48).

On the other hand, feedback that includes the positive characteristics outlined above produces gains in "teacher motivation, self-esteem, confidence, and sense of security" (Blase & Blase, 2004, pp. 143–144). Positive feedback is "potentially transforming" (Leithwood et al., 1999, p. 144). Feedback with positive elements is also associated with stronger school improvement measured in terms of student achievement gains (Mulford & Silins, 2003).

The other stem of appraisal support is praise and recognition (Hallinger & Heck, 1998), a construct heavily intertwined with feedback. Teachers consistently report that praise is of special importance, one of the most powerful tools that principals possess for affecting teachers and teaching (Blase & Kirby, 2009). Reviewers here find that "it is clear that effective principals build time for praise into their busy schedules" (p. 20)—an "ongoing support in the form of acknowledging others" (Gurr et al., 2006, p. 375). At times in the research, we see that recognition is expressed in terms of incentives and rewards (Leithwood et al., 2004), often in domains such as resources for professional development, career opportunities, and additional pay (Leitner, 1994; O'Donnell & White, 2005).

As was the case with feedback, there are elements that make praise work well or poorly. On the downside, leader praise is much less productive if it is laced with heavy doses of criticism. Praise that is seen as insensitive, inauthentic, or ritualistic is viewed by teachers as not helpful at best and harmful at worst. Fairness is seen as critical to teachers. When teachers perceive that principals are playing favorites, feedback often loses its meaning (Blase & Blase, 2004). It is the task of principals to pound meaning into praise. They move in this manner by providing praise that is "focused on specific and concrete teaching behaviors" (Blase & Blase, 2000, p. 136) and that is "being specific about what is being praised as 'good work'"(Leithwood et al., 1999, p. 73) and by using both public and private and formal and informal praise. Sincerity is a hallmark element of praise and recognition (Blase & Kirby, 2009). Public feedback should focus on individual and school-anchored achievements. Blase and Kirby (2009, p. 17) direct the spotlight to the essence of productive praise when they report that "teachers indicated that the praise that influenced them most was evoked by their work, that is, is related to professional performance."

As was the case with feedback, recognition is not an outcome in itself. At the group level, it is a tool for reinforcing school goals, building a positive school culture, promoting school reform, and improving student learning (Blase & Kirby, 2009; Leitner, 1994; Mayrowetz & Weinstein, 1999; Sather, 1999). On the individual front, scholars confirm that principal praise is linked to teacher pride, self-esteem, and efficacy (Blase & Blase, 1999). It has been linked to enhanced instructional performance. Specifically, praise has been shown to influence "teacher reflective behavior, including refinement of effective teaching strategies, risk taking, and innovation/ creativity" (Blase & Blase, 1999, p. 363).

Organizational Systems Support

As we saw with emotional and appraisal support, organizational systems support is comprised of various defining elements. One key element is buffering, finding ways to protect teachers from intrusions (Foster & St. Hilaire, 2003; Gray et al., 1999). Researchers over the last three decades have routinely found "that teachers in effective schools [are] buffered to a far greater extent than teachers in ineffective schools" (Rossmiller, 1992, p. 133). Leaders in effective schools see themselves as protectors (Supovitz & Poglinco, 2001). Particularly important is buffering the technical core (Leithwood et al., 1999) or "intrusions on teaching" (Riehl & Sipple, 1996, p. 883). On this topic, Leithwood, Day, Sammons, Harris, & Hopkins (2006, p. 37) remind us, "the buffering function acknowledges the open nature of schools and the constant bombardment of staff with expectations from parents, the media, special interest groups and the government."

Analysts of support via buffering expose an assortment of ways that principals protect teachers from intrusion. The core idea here is eliminating competing agendas (Bryk et al., 2010). One strategy is keeping required paperwork to a minimum (Lomotey, 1989). Another is not interrupting classes via the intercom systems or via messengers (Blase & Blase, 2004). A third is reducing teacher time committed to work outside their classrooms, especially meetings (Blase & Kirby, 2009). A fourth is "not burdening teachers with bureaucratic tasks and busy work" (Leithwood et al., 2011, p. 16) and "unreasonable demands from the policy environment (Leithwood et al., 2010, p. 678). Finally, buffering includes protecting "teachers from excessive pupil disciplinary activity" (Leithwood et al., 2006, p. 37). Like the other types of support examined above, buffering is linked to higher staff commitment to school goals (Riehl & Sipple, 1996).

Systems support is also about providing teachers with help when assistance is needed. Researchers affirm that both internal and external assistance are important (Louis & Miles, 1990). Helping teachers in implementing reforms is valuable (Louis & Miles, 1990). So, too, is securing mentoring assistance, especially for newly hired teachers (Youngs, 2007). The personal effort of the principal is noted across all the dimensions of assistance (Supovitz & Poglinco, 2001).

Systems support also includes the two pillars of methods of work and structures (Blanc et al., 2010; Jackson, 2000). Of particular importance here are the creation and use of collective decision making that promotes meaningful involvement, discretion, and authentic autonomy (not simply isolation) (Mangin, 2007; Murphy, 2005). Assorted scholars refer to this as "time and opportunities for peer connections among teachers" (Blase & Blase, 2000, p. 138), both during and outside the school day (Eilers & Camacho, 2007). Supovitz and Christman (2003, p. 7) conclude, for example, that

> Not only do communities need protected time that frees them to investigate instruction together, they also need structures to capitalize on the opportunities created by time together in order to have disciplined conversations about the connections between their instructional strategies and student learning.

Penuel and team (2009, 2010) conclude that social structure support is highly valuable in school implementation efforts, in energizing instructional change, and in generating "consistent forms of practice across a variety of settings" (2010, p. 87).

Structural systems that provide personal assistance to teachers, such as mentors and coaches are helpful (Huberman et al., 2011). Programs are also valuable (Auerbach, 2009). Noteworthy here are programs that create agreement on the boundaries of appropriate teaching practices, a reigning in of variation to enhance alignment and cohesion across classes (Newmann et al., 2001; Rowan & Miller, 2007). Operating schedules can also act as a form of systems support (McDougall, Saunders, & Goldenberg, 2007). Systems focused on "teaching workloads represent an[other] important resource that allows teachers to do their work" (Riehl & Sipple, 1996, p. 887). "Deploying staff creatively so as to keep classes as small as possible" (Cotton, 2003, p. 37) can be a powerful support (Newmann, Wehlage, & Lamburn, 1992). As we touched on above, attention is directed in the research to systems that provide teachers with support on student discipline issues (Blase & Kirby, 2009). In Chapter 6, we turn to the final piece of the capacity-building chronicle: talent development.

6

Talent Development

Talent development is a special type of support that is focused on building human capacity in schools. This human capital is comprised of the knowledge and skills possessed by teachers, what Bryk and team (2010, p. 108) refer to as "teachers' capacity to articulate engaging instructional pedagogy" and what Drago-Severson (2004) defines as the bundle of cognitive, interpersonal, and intrapersonal skills needed to function effectively.

There is a considerable paradox associated with efforts to enhance teacher capacity in schools. On the one hand, human capital is routinely described as perhaps the key element in the health of organizations and professions (Garet, Porter, Desimone, Birman, & Yoon, 2001; Tichy & Cardwell, 2004). Commitments of learning are essential, a precondition to individual and organizational growth (Porter, Garet, Desimone, & Birman, 2003; Scribner, Cockrell, Cockrell, & Valentine, 1999). Or as Blanc et al. (2010, p. 222) remind us, "[I]nvestments in human capital cannot be bypassed": "[O]rganizational improvement requires substantive and ongoing opportunities to learn" (Goldenberg, 2004, p. v).

In educational organizations, the same narrative is evident: (1) "Schools can do no better than the teachers who work in them" (Guskey, 2003, p. 16), (2) "school improvement and the improvement of teaching and student learning depend fundamentally on the development of teachers' knowledge [and] abilities" (Smylie, Conley, & Marks, 2002, p. 171), and (3) "improvement in the stock of teacher quality provides an important channel through which principals can raise the quality of education" (Branch, Hanushek, & Rivkin, 2012, p. 30). This conclusion holds for school change and systematic reform efforts (Blanc et al., 2010; Felner, Seitsinger,

Brand, Burns, & Bolton, 2007; Garet et al., 2001; Heller & Firestone, 1995) as well: "One cannot assume that schools can transform themselves into productive and successful places of learning without first addressing the learning that must occur among teachers" (Morrissey, 2000, p. 24) to enhance instruction. There is an axiom in schools: "If educators want to improve instruction then the skills of teachers must be upgraded" (Cooley & Shen, 2003, p. 18). And what holds for schools in general is of special importance for schools serving children placed at risk (Lomotey, 1989; Murphy, 2010).

In short, it is widely held that talent development is "the best bet for teaching practice" (Supovitz & Turner, 2000, p. 964), a conclusion confirmed in some of the best qualitative and quantitative research and scholarly reviews (Blase & Blase, 1999; Cotton, 2003; Hattie, 2009). Later in this section, we examine ways that principals broker capacity development and the accumulation of human capital. Here, we simply provide an advance organizer, confirming that "the most successful principals exhibit strong commitments to the professional development of the teaching staff" (Ross, Sterbinsky, & McDonald, 2003, pp. 18–19) and reinforcing the conclusion that "promoting teachers' professional development is the most influential instructional leadership behavior at both the elementary and high school levels" (Blase & Blase, 2004, p. 12).

On the other hand, although generally "touted as the ticket to reform" (Wilson & Berne, 1999, p. 185), professional development has enjoyed a checkered history in education (Hawley & Valli, 1999). Insufficient attention has been devoted to this critical domain of schooling. Traditional mechanisms are routinely found to be wanting, both at specific times in the life of schools and across the careers of teachers (Newmann, King, & Youngs, 2000; Palincsar, Magnusson, Marano, Ford, & Brown, 1998). "Schools generally do not have a coherent, coordinated approach to professional development" (Desimone, Porter, Garet, Yoon, & Birman, 2002, p. 105). They maintain a casual attitude that promotes dysfunctional norms such as isolation and privacy (Murphy, 2005). Much of the professional learning that has occurred has been "fragmented, intellectual superficial" and has failed "to take into account what we know about how teachers learn" (Borko, 2004, p. 3). Overall, the assessment is that "existing models of professional development are not adequate to achieve ambitious learning goals" (Supovitz & Turner, 2000, p. 964). We should not be surprised to discover a strategy with tremendous upside has not had the impact it could.

Over the last few decades, researchers and developers have helped us better grasp the construct of talent development by forging frameworks to discuss the research. Owen (2003) and others employ dimensions such as form, duration, content, collective participation, active learning, and coherence. Garet and colleagues (2001) portray five aspects of professional development under two major headers (core features and structural features). Borko (2004, p. 4), in turn, identifies the following as key components of professional development:

- the professional development program
- the teachers, who are the learners in the system
- the facilitator, who guides teachers as they construct new knowledge and practices
- the content in which the professional development occurs

In this chapter, we build from these assorted frameworks using three domains to capture the essentials of high-quality professional development: systems learning principles, adult learning principles, and community learning principles. We also spend considerable time examining the role of the principal in this arena.

PRINCIPLES OF TALENT DEVELOPMENT

Systems Learning Principles

On the systems front, research exposes a set of characteristics of effective professional development around the domain of time. To begin with, the central importance of time for learning to occur is consistently cited in the research (Firestone & Martinez, 2007; Goldenberg, 2004). We discern positive findings about subdimensions of time there as well. The importance of depth of learning experiences is visible across the literature (Barnes, Camburn, Sanders, & Sebastian, 2010; Penuel, Fishman, Yamaguchi, & Gallagher, 2007). For example, in their study, Supovitz and Turner (2000) found that dramatic results from professional development "emerged when the experiences were deep and more sustained. Both teaching practices and classroom cultures were affected most deeply after intensive and sustained staff development activities" (p. 975). Embedded here also is the time dimension of sustained work (Darling-Hammond & McLaughlin, 1995; Youngs & King, 2002). That is, "professional development is likely to be of higher quality if it is both sustained over time and involves a substantial number of hours" (Garet et al., 2001, p. 933). The research also exposes other related time dimensions that are important in the professional development algorithm, such as the span or the time period over which learning unfolds and the extensiveness of learning opportunities (Freiberg, Huzinec, & Templeton, 2009; Hawley & Valli, 1999). Follow-up time is critical as is time during the school day for learning activities (Blumenfeld, Fishman, Krajcik, Marx, & Soloway, 2000; Phillips, 2003). In short, quality professional development is a long-term endeavor (Goldenberg, 2004; McDougall, Saunders, & Goldenberg, 2007). The logic here is captured by Penuel and associates (2007): "Professional development that is of longer duration and time span is more likely to contain the kinds of learning opportunities necessary for teachers to integrate new knowledge into practice" (p. 929).

Researchers provide some specificity to these dimensions of time in their analyses. Joyce and Showers (cited in Freiberg et al., 2009, p. 75), for example, found that teachers require one year at a minimum to master a new curriculum. Supovitz and Turner (2000) concluded that teachers in their study required 80 hours of professional development before they began "using inquiry-based teaching practices significantly more frequently . . . than the average teacher" (p. 973). And significant change in the classroom culture occurred only after 160 hours of professional development.

Systems learning also provides insights about the coherence aspect of professional development. We know, for example, that capacity building is most productive when it is school based (Owen, 2003; Penuel et al., 2007). That is, it is "well matched to the school's needs" (Desimone et al., 2002, p. 449), "integral to school operations" (Hawley & Valli, 1999, p. 140), attends to learning within the school, and provides useful knowledge to teachers (Hawley & Valli, 1999; Hayes, Christie, Mills, & Lingard, 2004). We learn also that professional development is most productive when it "reflect[s] best demonstrable practice and [is] research based" (Hawley & Valli, 1999, p. 137), when the spotlight is on student learning goals and outcomes (Newmann et al., 2000; Youngs & King, 2002), and when it is "rooted in the knowledge base for teaching" (Wilson & Berne, 1999, p. 175). Likewise, effective capacity building is related to coherence among the activities, mission, and goals of the school; state and district standards; and the individual goals and needs of teachers (Garet et al., 2001; Leithwood, Jantzi, & Steinbach, 1999; Newmann et al., 2000; Owen, 2003). Researchers confirm that "activities that are connected to teachers' other professional development experiences and other reform efforts are more likely to produce enhanced knowledge and skills" (Garet et al., 2001, p. 933). In a similar vein, "a professional development activity is more likely to be effective in improving teachers' knowledge and skills if it forms a coherent part of a wider set of opportunities for teacher learning and development" (Garet et al., 2001, p. 927); that is, it "is integrated with a comprehensive change process that deals with the full range of impediments to and facilitators of student learning" (Hawley & Valli, 1999, p. 138).

More specifically, system learning reveals the importance of coherence of professional development with students' needs and "to what schools expect students to know and be able to do" (Hawley & Valli, 1999, p. 134). Coherence also addresses linkages to the results of teaching on children and to the processes by which children learn, including focus on specific youngsters (Garet et al., 2001; McLaughlin & Talbert, 2001; Robinson, 2007; Supovitz & Turner, 2000). Gravity here fuses professional development to "specific and concrete instrumental tasks" (McDougall et al., 2007, p. 85). On this issue, we know that professional development that "is integrated into the daily life of school is more likely to produce enhanced knowledge and skills" (Garet et al., 2001, p. 935). Palincsar and team (1998, p. 9) refer to this as "activity at the workbench" and "interactive with teaching practices" (Penuel et al., 2007, p. 929), while Owen (2003) calls these "practical ideas [that can be] incorporated directly into teaching" (p. 120). We also know that focus on content is an essential element of quality professional development (Garet et al., 2001). Research helps us see that "an explicit focus on subject matter" (Borko, 2004, p. 5) rather than on more general instructional practices defines effective professional development (Desimone, 2002). Indeed, Porter and associates (2003) conclude that "generic professional development that focuses on teaching techniques without a content focus does not appear to be effective" (p. 32). We return to the consequences of productive professional development. Here, we simply note that coherence has been linked to teacher knowledge, teacher change, curriculum implementation, and academic gains for students (Bryk et al., 2010; Garet et al., 2001; Penuel et al., 2007; Porter et al., 2003).

Principles of Adult Learning

We know that talent development has both individual and collective (community) dimensions (Borko, 2004). That is, "change in classroom teaching is a problem of individual learning as well as organizational learning" (Garet et al., 2001, p. 922). In this section, we concentrate on the former, examining the adult learning principles uncovered in studies of professional development that lead to important positive outcomes for teachers and children. In the following section, we redirect the spotlight to learning communities and principles that have important consequences for individuals and groups. As we will see, there is a unifying overlap between the individual and collective aspects of teacher learning, with the adult learning principles also playing out in community-based professional development (Stigler & Hiebert, 1999).

In the broadest sense, talent development "recognizes teachers as professionals and adult learners" (Wilson & Berne, 1999, p. 175). It is informed by and applies theories and principles of adult development (Blase & Blase, 2004; Drago-Severson, 2004). It is also "grounded in a common set of professional development standards" (Supovitz & Turner, 2000, p. 965). It begins with this reality: "One cannot assume that schools can transform themselves into productive and successful places of learning for students without first addressing the learning that must occur among teachers" (Morrissey, 2000, p. 24).

We learn also that impactful professional development fosters a sense of ownership for learning (Robinson, 2007). It is not the responsibility of others but an integral, self-regulated activity (Hawley & Valli, 1999). Learning depends less on control than on "teachers' personal and professional commitment to improve" (Blumenfeld et al., 2000, p. 156). Professional development scaffolded on adult learning principles underscores active learning and engaged learning opportunities (Desimone et al., 2002; Garet et al., 2001). According to Wilson and Berne (1999), this means "that teacher learning ought not to be bound and delivered but rather activated" (p. 194). "From this perspective, effective professional development programs would aim for more than transmitting knowledge [and] would also teach problem-solving knowledge in the work context" (Barnes et al., 2010, pp. 244–245). It includes more hands-on work than what is normal in the profession (Penuel et al., 2007). Learning has a robust generative dimension. It is constructed (Desimone et al., 2002; Franke, Carpenter, Levi, & Fennema, 2001).

Effective professional development is characterized by authenticity (Supovitz & Turner, 2000). Work is meaningful and relevant, not simply abstract (Blase & Blase, 2004; Desimone et al., 2002; Leithwood, Anderson, Mascall, & Strauss, 2011). It is practice based—"situated in classroom practice" (Wilson & Berne, 1999, p. 176)—and is "an integral part of the occupation and career of teaching" (Little, 1982, p. 334) in current time (Darling-Hammond & McLaughlin, 1995). Learning is about "actively wrestl[ing] with actual problems embedded in work" (Barnes et al., 2010, p. 244).

Talent development actions that are successful are practice anchored and job embedded; that is, they are context sensitive. *Context specificity* contains a number of key ideas but primarily, it means "building from analysis of [one's] own setting" (Hiebert & Pearson, 1999, p. 13). Sensitivity to context implies that "teachers learn in the classrooms and schools in which they teach" (Stigler & Hiebert, 1999, p. 135). They "learn how to teach more effectively while teaching" (Lyons & Pinnell, 1999, p. 205) rather than in traditional out-of-class sessions and school activities. Growth is "connected to and derived from teachers' work with children" (Askew & Gaffney, 1999, p. 87) and *effectiveness* comes to be defined in terms of "what works with the children [one is] teaching" (Duffy-Hester, 1999, p. 489; see also Pinnell, Lyons, DeFord, Bryk, & Seltzer, 1994). The center of gravity—that is, "resolving instructional problems" (Manning, 1995, p. 656)—is a real challenge in the classroom (Au & Asam, 1996). "All theory building is then checked against practice" (Askew & Gaffney, 1999, p. 85) and "application is direct and obvious" (Stigler & Hiebert, 1999, p. 165).

Impactful professional development "offer[s] a healthy mixture of both support and challenge (Drago-Severson, 2004, p. 33). Development based on the principles of adult learning challenges teachers' current understandings, creates productive disequilibrium, unfreezes current knowledge, "creat[es] opportunities for analysis and reflection" (Bryk et al., 2010, p. 55), and challenges problematic assumptions (Hawley & Valli, 1999; Robinson, 2007; Wilson & Berne, 1999). Challenge "push[es] the edges of a person's thinking and/or feeling so as to expose the person to new ways of thinking" (Drago-Severson, 2004, p. 33).

The above ideas underscore that there is a sense of localness about effective professional development (Anderson, Hiebert, Scott, & Wilkinson,

1985; Owen, 2003). We discern the importance of application and reflection (Barnes et al., 2010). Adult learning-based professional development is heavily inquiry based (Franke et al., 2001; Penuel et al., 2007). "Quality professional development immerse[s] participants in inquiry, questioning, and experimentation. [It] models inquiry forms of teaching" (Supovitz & Turner, 2000, p. 964). Just-in-time and ongoing feedback and reflection are distinctly visible (Garet et al., 2001; Owens, 2003). Professional development anchored in adult learning perspectives highlights the involvement of teachers in learning, including teacher input into the form, content, and activities of learning opportunities (Burch & Spillane, 2003; Hawley & Valli, 1999; Patty, Maschoff, & Ranson, 1996; Ruter, 1983). There is a fluidness and messiness to impactful professional development that belies the idea of tightly boxed learning (Hawley & Valli, 1999; Wilson & Berne, 1999). Because application of learning is critical, considerable attention is devoted to use of learning insights. Attention is also given to context, with particular emphasis on where teachers are in their professional careers (Drago-Severson, 2004). High-quality professional development is deeply embedded in the tapestry of the school and "learning is considered part of the work" (Hawley & Valli, 1999, p. 140). "Teachers are engaged in professional learning every day, all day long" (Owen, 2003, p. 103).

Community Learning Principles

A robust line of research confirms that much of the professional development in high-performing schools also has a collective focus, what Newmann and associates (2001) refer to as a *schoolwide focus*, Bryk and team (2010) call a *supportive professional work culture*, and Desimone and colleagues (2002) and Penuel and team (2007) describe as *collective participation*. That is,

> collective participation of groups of teachers from the same school, subject, or grade is related both to coherence and active learning opportunities, which in turn are related to improvements in teacher knowledge and skill and changes in classroom practice. (Garet et al., 2001, p. 936)

The spine of community-based learning principles is collegial action or communal arrangements (Askew & Gaffney, 1999). We also know that excellent schools "model a learning community in the way teachers engage with new learning to achieve common goals" (Bryk et al., 2010, p. 99). In short, community learning principles provide an invaluable framework for professional knowledge and growth, school improvement, teacher instruction, and student learning (Barnes et al., 2010; Bryk et al., 2010; Garet et al., 2001; McLaughlin & Talbert, 2001). "Without collaborative problem solving, individual change may be possible, but school change is not"

(Hawley & Valli, 1999, p. 141). Collaborative professional development works in straightforward ways. According to Penuel and colleagues (2009) and Mulford and Silins (2003), such efforts nurture the development of trust, enhance the acceptance of reform solutions, augment resources, motivate teachers, and provide clarity to change initiatives. Each, in turn, deepens the capacity for learning.

CAUTIONS

There are some important cautions to be surfaced here, however. First, the learning community is not a panacea (Bryk et al., 2010; Supovitz & Christman, 2003). "There is nothing particularly virtuous about collaboration per se. Individuals can collaborate to block change or inhibit progress just as easily as they can enhance the process" (Guskey, 2003, p. 12).

Thus, one of the most critical concerns is a misguided faith in the ability of structure and policy to power change (Murphy, 1991). Specifically, by ignoring the tendency for reforms to materialize sans engine and drive train, we often end up with a change in name only (McLaughlin & Talbert, 2001). In this case, that would be a group of teachers bound together by time but without the trust, vision, resources, and responsibility to transform into a community (Penuel et al., 2009; Youngs, 2007).

While we often describe this in terms of the creation of an *empty shell*, a second, in-name-only problem needs to be surfaced. We refer to the formation of inauthentic, artificial, or pseudo community (Grossman, Wineburg, & Woolworth, 2001; Vescio, Ross, & Adams, 2008). Pseudo community may actually be more harmful than the empty-shell structure because it has the potential to actively solidify nonproductive patterns of interactions among teachers, such as burying conflicts and problems and silencing joint exchange (Grossman et al., 2001; Hoy, Hannum, & Tschannen-Moran, 1998).

Second, teacher learning communities are defined by universal ideas (e.g., collective responsibility). But this does not mean that getting those principles and norms into play is the same in all situations (Supovitz, 2008; Vescio et al., 2008). As Craig (2009) reminds us, community work "fuses[s] or collide[s] with the mixture of what is already going on" (p. 615). The cost of overlooking context in the area of learning communities is especially high (Walker & Slear, 2011). We know that "teachers bring their own contexts with them" to the community (Penuel et al., 2007, p. 931). We also know subject matter is important in the community-building process (Burch & Spillane, 2003; McLaughlin & Talbert, 2001). That is, subject-matter norms will mediate how teachers think about and respond to community-building initiatives. The obvious corollary is that the department context matters for practice communities (Siskin, 1994; Stoll, Bolam, McMahon, Wallace, & Thomas, 2006). History matters as well, as does the existing stock of relational trust (Bryk et al., 2010; Kochanek, 2005). Level of schooling is important (McLaughlin & Talbert, 2001; Moller & Eggen, 2005). District context and school size exert influence over community development (Dannetta, 2002; Louis, 2007). Personal characteristics such as gender, race, and years of experience also shape the formation of professional communities (Grissom & Keiser, 2011; Visscher & Witziers, 2004).

Third, there is the possibility that a practice community will misfire, producing negative results (Curry, 2008; Grossman et al., 2001). For example, researchers have documented how learning communities can negatively operate: (1) "to perpetuate stereotypes, prejudice, and staid or destructive practices" (Printy, 2008, p. 188); (2) to reinforce exclusion, insularity, and marginalization; (3) to herald the status quo and staunch innovation; (4) to nurture dysfunctional relationships; and (5) to privilege management goals at the expense of professional objectives (Hayes et al., 2004; McLaughlin & Talbert, 2001; Smylie & Hart, 1999; Stoll et al., 2006).

One emerging concern is that communities will become vehicles to engage work unrelated to mission in much the same way that guidance counselors have been transformed into quasi-administrators at times. That is, teachers in communities will work on everything but instructional practice, leading to a type of administrative usurpation and organizational goal displacement (Firestone & Martinez, 2007; Penuel et al., 2010; Supovitz, 2002). Another growing worry is that these professional communities will simply bury teachers under the weight of added responsibilities (Murphy, 2005; Webb, 2005). More bothersome is some evidence that the downsides of open dialogue and constructive critical conversations can be unleashed in professional communities; that is, "community can have ambivalent as well as positive tendencies" (King, 2001, p. 247). Tensions and anxieties are often toxic byproducts of learning communities (Mullen & Hutinger, 2008).

It is also appropriate here to remind ourselves that once in place, communities are often fragile (Palincsar et al., 1998; Printy, 2008). Regression to old patterns of behavior and norms is not unusual (Goldstein, 2004). Thus, cautions about stalling out merit scrutiny as well (Greene & Lee, 2006; Levine & Marcus, 2007).

COLLABORATION AS THE CENTER PILLAR

As introduced above, communities of practice are defined by the norm of collaboration (Blase & Blase, 2000; Ross et al., 2003). Ermeling (2010) defines collaboration as a "joint productive activity where participants assist each other to solve a common problem or produce a common product" (p. 386). Because it is more tangible than other elements of community and often provides the backdrop on which the elements come to life, it occupies disproportionate space in the community of practice narrative.

For collaboration to be productive, shifts in how teachers think about, talk about, and go about their work are required (Drago-Severson, 2004; Levine & Marcus, 2010). It rests on the understanding that what teachers do outside their classrooms is as important as what unfolds inside those settings and that collective work done well can accelerate their learning and the achievement of their students (Heck & Hallinger, 2009; McLaughlin & Talbert, 2001; Stoll et al., 2006; Supovitz, 2002).

An assortment of researchers have crafted robust frameworks to expose the aspects of collaboration. For example, for McLaughlin and Talbert (2001), "teachers are mutually engaged in teaching; they jointly develop their practice; and they share a repertoire of resources and history" (p. 41). For Printy (2008), the following are all important pieces of collaborative effort: "the range of activities available for participation, the quality of members' participation as legitimate or peripheral, the rules for social interaction of members, and the joint understanding of the work that brings individuals together" (p. 199). More generally, Wenger (1998, 2000) describes collaboration as an algorithm of events, commitments, membership, and tasks. From our analysis, we assert that the power of professional communities of practice can be measured by how well the sub-elements of engagement—purpose, structure, focus, and nature— adhere to known quality criteria. More concretely, we find that effective collaboration is mutual, purpose-driven work. It is learning centered and instructionally focused. It is driven by the tenets of evidence-based inquiry. And it is directed to improved teacher practice and student achievement via teacher learning (Murphy & Torre, 2014).

Purpose

Effective collaboration is defined by clear purpose, "persistently working toward detectable improvements" (Ermeling, 2010, p. 378). The work itself is the avenue to improvement, not the outcome. Effectiveness plays out in the application of a teacher's learning practice (Cochran-Smith & Lytle, 1999). What Wenger (1998, 2000) refers to as the "purpose of shared enterprise" (1998, p. 45) pivots on clear measures of outcomes benchmarked against expectations or common goals and compelling direction (Fullan, 2002; Johnson & Asera, 1999; Louis, 2007).

Mutuality provides the structure or frame of collaboration, the process of joint work (Johnson & Asera, 1999; Supovitz, 2010). It is grounded on the understanding that relationships are the heart and soul of community (Bryk et al., 2010; Gronn, 2009). One of the fathers of communities of practice, Wenger, talks about "mutual engagement" (2000, p. 229) and "shared enterprise" (1998, p. 45). Colleagues in education refer to mutuality as *group practice*, changing a roster of individuals into a collaboration of "relational cultures" (Drago-Severson, 2004, p. 40), "joint enterprise" (Young, 2006, p. 538), and "joint identity" (Grossman et al., 2001, p. 63) featuring a "culture of collaboration" (Southworth, 2002, p. 88), "collective engagement" (Visscher & Witziers, 2004, p. 786), and a "process of participation" (Horn, 2005, p. 211).

Mutuality, according to Printy (2008), requires that members be advantaged by access to the resources of the group and that they add to that capacity (Heller & Firestone, 1995; McLaughlin & Talbert, 2001). It is about "enabling a rich fabric of connectivity" (Wenger, 2000, p. 232). It is about making shared engagement, peer support, mutual assistance, and joint enterprise a generalized condition in schools and about working and learning together (Goldenberg, 2004; Kruse, Seashore Louis, & Bryk, 1995; Olivier & Hipp, 2006; Stein & Coburn, 2008). It is about active engagement in "meaningful discussion, planning, and practice" (Garet et al., 2001, p. 925). Mutuality is essential because it "provides a point of convergence for teachers' inquiry—the joint enterprise for community of practice" (McLaughlin & Talbert, 2001, p. 122). It underscores needed job-centered learning and fosters capacity development (Clark, Dyson, Millward, & Robson, 1999; Drago-Severson, 2004; Olivier & Hipp, 2006). Shared enterprise features what Louis and Marks (1998) refer to as "the quality of relationships among group work members" (p. 538). Collegial support and general norms of teamwork and joint engagement are paramount under conditions of mutuality (Grossman et al., 2001; Phillips, 2003). Without mutuality, purpose of engagement cannot be fulfilled (Levine & Marcus, 2010).

Mutuality and its family members—participation, engagement, and joint activity—are dependent, of course, on opportunities to work together, on "enabling structure and supportive organizational context" (Fullan, 2002, p. 15) or "knowledge space" (Hattie, 2009, p. 264). These opportunities are often conspicuous by their absence in schools and require the strong hand of leadership broadly defined. Of course, this means that there needs to be something on which time to plan, work, and learn together makes sense (Johnson & Asera, 1999), "some intersection of interest, some activity" (Wenger, 2000, p. 232), what Ermeling (2010) refers to as "common ground to talk" (p. 386). Without this, there can be no authentic joint exchange (Beck & Foster, 1999; Hawley & Valli, 1999).

Structure

Creating structure for productive joint enterprise requires attending to an array of issues. Most importantly, there is the need to establish the domain of collaboration (Wenger & Snyder, 2000). We know also that thought must be devoted to what Wenger (2000) refers to as the types of activities that will ground the collaborative. Important here is ensuring that both formal and informal mechanisms are engaged in a coordinated and synchronized manner (Ancess, 2003; Drago-Severson, 2004; Olivier & Hipp, 2006). The size of groups is important and the question of how much to align with existing organizational arrangements (e.g., departments, grade levels, teaching teams) needs consideration (Wenger, 1998, 2000). Thus, the topic of boundaries is important, including how these demarcations are managed (Penuel et al., 2010; Wenger, 2000). So, too, is the fluidity and stability of collaborative work teams, what Wenger (2000) describes as rhythms of the work (Curry, 2008; McLaughlin & Talbert, 2001). Amount of time to work and the regularity of exchanges also merit consideration. So does the life span of a work group (Leithwood et al., 1999; McLaughlin & Talbert, 2001). The topic of how teachers become members of collaborative teams also must be addressed. Contrary to normal practice in education, self-selection receives high grades in the general literature as a mechanism of selection (Wenger, 1998). Also important is how much of one's professional identity is committed to and defined by collaborative work (Wenger, 2000). Finally, research informs us that how work is structured and the tools employed to guide the work make valuable contributions to how well joint enterprise is conducted (Levine & Marcus, 2010; Saunders, Goldenberg, & Gallimore, 2009). The concreteness of the work and the collaborative organizational form employed are quite relevant as well (Vescio et al., 2008).

The research carries us one level deeper in thinking about collaboration to the criteria for judging the authenticity of joint work. Issues here include the presence or absence of reciprocal influence, the density of ties, and mutual dependence (Beck & Foster, 1999; Kruse et al., 1995; Young, 2006; Wenger, 2000). Measures of the amount of the teaching-learning process (i.e., the work of classrooms) that is made open for inspection helps determine authenticity; that is, how much of the work becomes "public" (Grossman et al., 2001; Horn, 2005; Printy, 2008; Young, 2006). The depth of sharing can reveal a good deal about the validity of collaboration (Harris, 2009; Young, 2006). The "fingerprint" test for joint construction work is useful here. How many members of the collaborative actively contributed to the work? How many were mere spectators? Authenticity can also be determined in part by the robustness of the leadership displayed by members in the collaborative (Murphy, 2005). The extent to which teachers change their practice is a key criterion (Printy, 2008; Visscher & Witziers, 2004). We revisit many of these issues below when we examine specific responsibilities of principals in collaborative community work.

Focus

Structure is an essential dimension of all support and of community in particular. But as Ancess (2003) cautions, "[A]chievement of community requires more than the space for developing commodity" (p. 4). More specifically, "what collaboration is designed to focus on will have significant implications for what teachers can and can't learn from work with colleagues" (Levine & Marcus, 2010, pp. 392–393). For example, researchers report that simply addressing logistical issues and non-learning conditions does not translate into robust collaboration and community nor result in intermediate or summative outcomes.

On the positive side of the storyboard, analysts have uncovered productive foci for collaborative work. To begin with, it is clear that the center of gravity should be the classroom and on challenges of work there (Gray et al., 1999; Hayes et al., 2004). Educational concerns trump nonacademic issues (Murphy, Beck, Crawford, & Hodges, 2001). Attention flows to the core technology (Mulford & Silins, 2003; Useem, Christman, Gold, & Simon, 1997). That is, interactions should be anchored in issues of learning and teaching and be deep and ongoing (Supovitz, Sirinides, & May, 2010; Useem et al., 1997).

Not surprisingly, given the above comments, there is near-universal agreement that the focus of collaborative engagement should be on students (Ancess, 2003; Ermeling, 2010). For teachers to both mature into a productive community and power up learning, students need to be at the center of collaborative work (Goldenberg, 2004; Grossman et al., 2001). Becoming more specific, these analysts find that the focus should be on student academics (Olivier & Hipp, 2006; Saunders et al., 2009): "A collective focus on student learning is central to professional community" (Louis & Marks, 1998, p. 539), especially analyses of students' learning needs, problems, and progress (Halverson, Grigg, Prichett, & Thomas, 2007; Vescio et al., 2008). There is a "shared understanding of teaching and learning" (Bryk et al., 2010, p. 133) and shared language (Hawley & Villa, 1999).

By backward mapping from student learning, we find that the focus of this collective engagement is instructional practice embedded in specific curricular domains, collaboration to strengthen the school's instructional program and the pedagogical skills of each teacher (Curry, 2008; Gurr, Drysdale, & Mulford, 2006; Huberman, Parrish, Hannan, Arellanes, & Shambaugh, 2011; McLaughlin & Talbert, 2001; Supovitz & Poglinco, 2001; Young, 2006). Vescio and colleagues (2008) succinctly summarize the research on this issue as follows: "Findings reinforce the importance of persistently pursuing an instructional focus as teachers engage in their work in learning communities" (p. 85). As discussed above, a "problems of practice" focus is privileged in highly productive collaborative work (Levine & Marcus, 2010; McLaughlin & Talbert, 2001). The spotlight is on specific, observable, malleable practices that are described with transparency, clarity, and concreteness (Little, 1982; Mitchell & Sackney, 2006), a "collaborative examination of day-to-day practice" (Vescio et al., 2008, p. 81). Finally, as we explain more fully below, a particular type of shared instructional practice is routinely discussed in the research on teacher communities in general and collaboration, particularly evidence-based analysis (Blanc et al., 2010; Cosner, 2011), a condition that Visscher and Witziers (2004) refer to as the "sine qua non for the development of professional communities" (p. 798).

Nature

So far, we have examined three of the four core ingredients of collaboration (purpose, structure, and focus). We now turn to the final aspect of shared enterprise, the ways in which productive communities operate. To maintain consistency with colleagues who have researched this domain, we will describe the method of engagement as *reflective practice* (Blase & Blase, 2004). According to Stoll and her team (2006, pp. 222–227):

> *Reflective professional inquiry* includes: "reflective dialogue" conversations about serious educational issues or problems involving the application of new knowledge in a sustained manner; "deprivatization of practice," frequent examining of teachers' practice through mutual observation and case analysis, joint planning, and curriculum development; seeking new knowledge; tacit knowledge constantly converted into shared knowledge through interaction; and applying new ideas and information to problem solving and solutions addressing pupils' needs.

We parcel the research on *method of engagement* into two overlapping concepts: inquiry and evidence-based practice.

On the first topic, in dissecting collaboration, scholars consistently highlight professional practice informed by individual and group reflection (Grossman et al., 2001; Louis, Dretzke, & Wahlstrom, 2010). Indeed, inquiry is generally presented as a hallmark method or stance that defines shared enterprise in communities of practice (Grossman et al., 2001; Visscher & Witziers, 2004). The concept travels under a variety of different names in the literature—*reflective inquiry, reflective discussions, group inquiry, sustained inquiry, inquiry-oriented practice, reflective practice, collegial inquiry*, and so forth. It means, according to Drago-Severson (2004, p. 18), "reflecting on one's assumptions, convictions, and values as part of the learning process" or, as King (2001) describes, the investigation and critical assessment of practice, research, and logic. That is, it is a stance that honors the interrogation of knowledge, skills, and dispositions around instructional practice (Levine & Marcus, 2007). Its purpose is to forge joint understanding of and shared practices in the service of student learning (Kruse et al., 1995; Mitchell & Sackney, 2006). Productive inquiry in professional communities of practice is analytic, dynamic, continuous, and constructivist in nature (Horn, 2005; Little, 1982).

Reflective inquiry has as much to do with *dialogue*, what Horn (2005, p. 229) calls "conversational involvement," as it does with patterns of thinking (Stoll et al., 2006; York-Barr & Duke, 2004). Indeed, it is reasonable to add conversation to the methods of engagement label, what Wilson and Berne (1999, p. 200) nicely capture with the term "narrative of inquiry." Grossman and her colleagues (2001, p. 59) maintain that teacher communities create an "invitational conversational climate," a reflective-based constructed dialogue, what Cochran-Smith and Lytle (1999, p. 280) nail with the idea of "teacher learning through talk." It is in these continuous professional conversations that reflections become visible for inspection, venues in which feedback can be provided and debated (Curry, 2008; Kruse et al., 1995).

Two aspects of dialogue in the service of building collaboration are routinely highlighted in the research on professional culture. The public nature of conversations is consistently seen as essential, what Levine and Marcus (2010) describe as detailed and open representations (Horn, 2010; Young, 2006). This public stance centered on student work is especially productive (Goldenberg, 2004). A good deal of recognition is also awarded to the openness of collaborative exchange (Garet et al., 2001), an idea that Horn (2010, p. 255) beautifully captures as "a willingness to reveal and work at the limits of one's knowledge." Dialogue is not merely an act of civility. Difficult conversations unfold in collaborative work (Drago-Severson, 2004; Huberman et al., 2011). Critique is expected (Grossman et al., 2001; Silins & Mulford, 2004). "Questioning and challenging colleagues" is normal (Horn, 2010, p. 234). Concerns and doubts are to be aired and "difference, debate, and disagreement are viewed as the foundations" of reflective inquiry (Stoll et al., 2006, p. 227). In addition, there is solid evidence that formalizing collaborative conversations in education can be helpful (Beachum & Dentith, 2004; Levine & Marcus, 2010). There is a strong sense that "protocol-guided conversations" (Curry, 2008, p. 742) enhance the public and critical aspects of collaborative dialogue (Horn, 2005).

Collegial dialogue is half of the method or stance on engagement. The other half, based on the findings of Levine and Marcus (2010) and Penuel and colleagues (2006, p. 527) that "the effectiveness of collaboration depends on what kinds of interactions take place," is evidence based (Fullan & Ballew, 2002; Grossman et al., 2001). This means that not only is there critical, collegial exchange but the conversations are anchored in knowledge and data, especially support for ideas and—more importantly—evidence of impact on one's students (Ermeling, 2010; Hattie, 2009).

In highly productive collaboratives, considerable attention is devoted to the "visible and explicit cause-effect connections between instructional decisions and student outcomes" (Ermeling, 2010, p. 379). "Analysis and interpretation of some form of student learning data" (Cosner, 2011, p. 789) is the grist for collaborative dialogue (Visscher & Witziers, 2004). As was the case for inquiry, researchers find that tools such as protocols and artifacts to guide evidence-based collaboration can assist greatly in the work (Horn, 2005).

TYPES OF PROFESSIONAL DEVELOPMENT

As we have documented above, building capacity of existing staff is about bringing to life systems learning principles, adult learning principles, and community learning principles, almost always in an integrated manner. In this section, we spotlight the ways in which capacity building takes form.

At the macro level, reviewers discuss both "linking teachers to external assistance and creating internal conditions that support teacher development" (Youngs & King, 2002, p. 656). They also routinely emphasize both the formal and informal modes of learning (Johnson & Asera, 1999; Leithwood & Jantzi, 2006). A two-dimensional perspective that divides professional development into those focused on individual teachers and those attending to collaborative work is also well established in the research (Bulkley & Hicks, 2005; McLaughlin & Talbert, 2001). Ross and team (2003), also highlighting the macro level, divide professional development in these two aspects: "encouraging teachers to attend training sessions and enabling teachers to meet during school and provide support to each other" (p. 23). Similarly, Saunders and associates (2009) divide professional development into "two engagements, learning teams and conventional professional development" (p. 1029). In their seminal study, Porter and colleagues (2003) discuss both traditional activities (e.g., workshops) and reform activities (e.g., action research teams). Drago-Severson (2004) distinguishes

> between transformational learning—learning that helps adults to develop capacities to better manage the complexities of work and life—and informational learning—increases in knowledge and skills that are also important and can support changes in adults' attitudes and possibly their competencies. (p. 23)

Ancess (2000) deepens this framework by categorizing learning experiences into those where teachers generate or construct new knowledge and those where they reproduce knowledge.

Hawley and Valli (1999) provide a framework that features five models of professional development, including the individually guided model, the training model, the observer assessment model, the development/improvement process model, and the teacher researcher model. Drago-Severson (2004) posits a six-part architecture: training; observation/coaching/assessment; improvement process; inquiry and collaborative action research; self-directed; and mentoring.

Blase and Blase's (1999) investigation linking leadership and professional development produced six professional development strategies:

> (a) emphasizing the study of teaching and learning; (b) supporting collaboration efforts among educators; (c) developing coaching relationships among educators; (d) encouraging and supporting redesign of programs; (e) applying the principles of adult learning, growth, and development to all phases of staff development; and (f) implementing action research to inform instructional decision making. (p. 361)

Also, by focusing on leaders directly, Drago-Severson (2004) found that

> principals employ four mutually reinforcing initiatives that support adult growth and development; they form the four pillars on which the weight of this new learning-oriented model rests. They are (1) teaming/partnering with colleagues within and outside of the school, (2) providing teachers with leadership roles, (3) engaging in collegial inquiry, and (4) mentoring. (p. 17)

Cochran-Smith and Lytle (1999) provide an especially insightful and helpful set of conceptions in the area of teacher learning featuring knowledge of practice. The framework is especially useful because it addresses the key elements of what, how, and why teachers learn. These scholars unpack three conceptions of teacher learning. The first is *knowledge for practice*. Here, the focus is on the external generation of knowledge that teachers then employ to improve teaching. The second is *knowledge in practice*. Here, we see that "the most essential knowledge is practical knowledge," knowledge "embedded in practice and in teachers' reflections on practice" (p. 250). The third conception is *knowledge of practice*. Here, the assumption is "that the knowledge teachers need to teach well emanates from systematic inquiries about teaching, learners and learning, [and] subject matter and curriculum. The knowledge is constructed collectively" (p. 274).

At the micro level, analysts catalogue the types of experiences in which/with which teachers participate. The list is long and covers important activities such as professional development workshops, university-offered classes, mentoring relationships, opportunities to work with colleagues, action research projects, dissemination of written materials such as articles and protocols, opportunities to observe and to be observed by colleagues at one's school, visits to other sites, coaching, guided professional readings, and opportunities to lead in one's school or district (Cotton, 2003; Owen, 2003).

Below, we turn our attention more explicitly to the role of principals in making the architecture and forms of teacher learning productive in their schools. Before we do so, however, we highlight four contextual notes. First, as Hattie (2009) has documented, not all forms of professional development are equal in their impact on teacher knowledge and instructional practice:

> The four types of instruction found to be most effective on teacher knowledge and behavior were observation of actual classroom methods; microteaching; video-audio feedback; and practice. Lowest effects were from discussion, lectures, games/simulations, and guided field trips. Coaching, modeling, and production of printed or instructional materials also had lower effects. (p. 120)

Second, not all teachers benefit equally from professional learning opportunities. For example, Hill and colleagues (2005)

> suggest that those who may benefit most are teachers in the lowest third of the distribution of knowledge and that efforts to recruit teachers into professional development and preservice coursework might focus most heavily on those with weak subject matter knowledge for teaching. (p. 400)

Third, learning type is a holding container that does not make the topic of quality obvious. Other aspects of professional development need to be added to the narrative as well (Anderson, Moore, & Sun, 2009). To improve professional development, it is more important to focus on the duration, collective participation, and the core features (i.e., content, active learning, and coherence) than type (Garet et al., 2001, p. 936). Fourth, we need to remember that regardless of type, professional development works best when it is in the service of goals and school reforms and when it is part of a coherent and integrated system of school improvement (Bryk et al., 2010; Hawley & Valli, 1999; Newmann et al., 2000). Two of the most significant studies of the last 20 years make these points quite explicitly:

> High-quality professional development in the context of a supportive professional community and where teachers were oriented toward improvement appears powerfully related to gains in academic productivity. (Bryk et al., 2010, p. 113)

> This suggests that compared to teachers whose professional development is not coherent, teachers who experience professional development that is coherent—that is, connected to their other professional development experiences, aligned with standards and assessments, and fosters professional communication—are more likely to change their practice. This positive effect for teachers whose professional development is coherent is true even compared to teachers who have gained the same underlying knowledge and skills as a result of their professional development experiences. (Garet et al., 2001, p. 934)

EXPLICIT NOTES ON THE ROLE OF THE PRINCIPAL IN PROFESSIONAL DEVELOPMENT

In an earlier section, we described three dimensions of professional development—system learning principles, adult learning principles, and community learning principles. We expand on that work in this section by making explicit what leaders in effective schools do to promote teacher learning. We begin with general insights about the principal and then examine what researchers tell us about the activities of leaders in the area of communities of professional practice.

The General Role

Three points ground our analysis. First, promoting teacher learning is one of the most, if not *the* most, powerful leverage points in the portfolio leaders have to promote school improvement and increase student learning (Askew, Fountas, Lyons, Pinnell, & Schmitt, 2000; Rowe, 1995). In a major review, for example, Cotton (2003) discovered that "[p]rincipals of high-achieving schools offer more, and more varied, professional development activities than those in lower achieving schools. They are creative in securing the resources—financial, human, time, materials, and facilities—the school needs to improve" (p. 71).

In a second major review, Robinson (2007) concludes that the large impact here offers "empirical support for calls to school leaders to be actively involved with their teachers as the 'leading learners' of their schools" (pp. 15–16). And Newmann and team (2000) find a "powerful positive association between comprehensive professional development and the extent to which the principal exerts leadership" (p. 283).

Second, the salience of principals in this domain is heightened by the fact that the critical elements of learning are almost impossible to bring forth "in the absence of leadership initiative" (Leithwood et al., 1999, p. 150)—"building professional capacity requires principal support" (Heck & Hallinger, n.d., p. 31). Teachers cannot pull this off on their own. Third, we reintroduce the caveat that leadership can also flummox the domain of teacher learning. Leadership can be "counterproductive if it is done without reference to the evidence about the particular qualities and processes of teacher professional development that produce effects on the students of participating teachers" (Robinson, Lloyd, & Rowe, 2008, p. 669).

One aspect of the good news here is that there are a variety of ways that leaders can bolster and enhance teacher learning and development. Major frameworks (some of which include actions in the area of professional community that we address below) have been provided by Drago-Severson (2004), who describes four pillars or "mutually reinforcing initiatives that support adult growth and development" (p. 17). They include (1) teaching/partnering with colleagues within and outside of the school, (2) providing teachers with leadership roles, (3) engaging in collegial inquiry, and (4) mentoring. Blase and Blase (2000, p. 135) describe six strategies principals in their studies employed to promote teacher learning:

(1) emphasizing the study of teaching and learning

(2) supporting collaboration efforts among educators

(3) developing coaching relationships among educators

(4) encouraging and supporting redesign of programs

(5) applying the principles of adult learning, growth, and development to all phases of staff development

(6) implementing action research to inform instructional decision making

Youngs and King (2002) suggest, in turn,

that effective principals can sustain high levels of capacity by establishing trust, creating structures that promote teacher learning, and either (a) connecting their faculties to external expertise or (b) helping teachers generate reforms internally. (p. 665)

And Leithwood and associates (1999) point out in their extensive review that leadership contributes to teacher learning and growth when school principals

- ensure that adequate financial, time, personnel, materials, and other resources necessary to support teacher development activities are available;
- provide opportunities for teachers to develop a shared view of the school's overall mission and more specific goals to which they are strongly committed;
- help teachers assess their own needs for growth and gain access to sources of assistance inside or outside the school;
- foster the development of a collaborative school culture within which opportunities exist for authentic participation in decision making about school improvement efforts and meaningful interaction with colleagues about collective purposes and how to achieve them;
- build feelings of self-efficacy by recognizing teachers' accomplishments and by providing support to help reduce anxiety about tackling new initiatives; and
- share or distribute the responsibility for teacher development broadly throughout the school—for example, to teachers' colleagues, to teachers themselves, to external people who may be assisting in the school improvement effort, and to the school improvement initiative in which teachers are engaged. (p. 161)

While many principals "are involved only in the mechanical arrangements" of professional development (Leithwood & Montgomery, 1982, p. 327), principals in high-performing schools understand the value of teacher learning and honor that value in their work (Dinham, 2005; Youngs & King, 2002). They demonstrate deep personal involvement in the learning of adults. Or, as Useem and colleagues (1997) remind us, "[T]he impact of professional development initiatives on a school [is] conditional to a large extent by the degree to which principals themselves become part of a collegial effort" (p. 68). Principals in high-performing schools expend more time on the professional development of teachers than do typical principals who "allocate very little of their time to activities aimed at improving teachers' teaching skills" (Heck, 1992, p. 30). They make "support for adult learning a demonstrated personal priority" (Drago-Severson, 2004, p. 4). Equally important, because one cannot lead what one does not know, effective principals build commitment to and involvement in professional development on a deep understanding of instruction, curriculum, and assessment (Coldren & Spillane, 2007; Nelson & Sassi, 2005).

Principals in high-performing schools are also strong catalysts for teacher learning (Bryk et al., 2010). They are out and about the school, encouraging teachers in their efforts to grow. They encourage teachers to open their doors to colleagues inside and outside the school (Eilers & Camacho, 2007) and support them in becoming resources for their colleagues as well, what Anderson and team (2009) call "residential experts" (p. 123). They provide a good deal of sensemaking to the work in and around teacher learning. These leaders are powerful facilitators as well. They "understand [that] professional development can be a difficult journey that requires courage, risk taking, and even some failure along the way" (Blase & Blase, 1999, p. 18). Because of this, they are active in building bridges to learners and facilitating teachers' learning of content knowledge (Supovitz & Poglinco, 2001). And they incentivize and acknowledge teachers for their learning activities (Spillane, Diamond, Walker, Halverson, & Jita, 2001) and "remove penalties for making mistakes as part of efforts toward professional improvement" (Leithwood et al., 1999, p. 76). As we reported in the area of support in general, a good deal of the principal's efforts here is centered around time and structural and material assistance (Owen, 2003).

Effective leaders make active investments in the professional learning of teachers in their schools (Hiebert & Pearson, 1999). These principals "provide the monetary or the other types of resources required to support teacher development activities" (Leithwood et al., 1999, p. 161). "They earmark resources for the professional development" of teachers (Cotton, 2000, p. 14). They release staff to pursue learning opportunities that will benefit their students (Bryk et al., 2010; Dinham, 2005). They secure substitutes to cover release time for learning (Heller & Firestone, 1995; Timperley, 2009) so that teachers can "observe other teachers' classrooms and work with outside staff developers" (Bryk et al., 2010, p. 214). High-performing principals "help teachers gain access to sources of assistance inside or outside the school" as necessary (p. 161).

The research informs us that more effective principals demonstrate a hands-on or personal touch on professional development (Grissom, Loeb, & Master, n.d.; Manning 1995; Samuels, 1981). They spend more time than the average principal interacting informally around issues of learning for teachers (Burch & Spillane, 2003). They are also "more likely to be described by their teachers as participating in informal staff discussion of teaching and teaching problems" (Robinson et al., 2008, p. 663). They exercise a more consultative stance with their teachers (Youngs & King, 2002). Analysts also routinely report that effective leaders model what they expect their teacher colleagues to do (Dinham, 2005; Leithwood et al., 1999). They lead with action, not simply exhortation. They personally demonstrate the values and principles of quality professional development, especially the habit of "modeling continual learning in [their] own practice" (Mulford & Silins, 2003, p. 179). Nelson and Sassi (2005) capture this beautifully when they tell us that these principals "open themselves up to be learners as well as leaders" (p. 174). We also know that "modeling the importance of learning while leading is one way that principals build a healthy school climate" (Drago-Severson, 2004, p. 50).

Effective leaders promote learning "by widening the compass of leadership potential" (MacBeath, 2009, p. 49) in their schools and by helping teachers assume leadership roles (Spillane et al., 2001). Leaders in effective schools tend to be active participants with teachers in learning opportunities (Cotton, 2003; Robinson, 2007), "participat[ing] more consistently in meetings and teachers professional development sessions than principals at comparison schools" (McDougall et al., 2007, p. 70). They are also more active in presenting to their staff in groups and working one-on-one with teachers in their classrooms (O'Donnell & White, 2005; Sweeney, 1982). They become "fellows in communities of learners and activists for professional learning" (Mullen & Hutinger, 2008, p. 280). Such personal involvement seems to enhance the value of professional development activities by communicating something important to teachers (Blase & Blase, 2004; Datnow & Castellano, 2001).

The Role of the Principal in Professional Development via Learning Communities

Although we possess less knowledge than we might desire, we have accumulated understandings about principals and learning communities over the last 20 years, some of which stretch across the more general findings just examined. We know, for example, that there are a set of key domains in which preemptive prevention, removal of existing barriers, and/or the construction of an infrastructure to support professional communities occur. We also understand now that the principal has a hallmark position in this work, a conclusion found in nearly every study of teacher communities of practice (Cosner, 2011; Halverson et al., 2007; Louis et al., 2010; Mitchell & Sackney, 2006; Stoll et al., 2006). We are aware that there are important differences in the shape and texture of leadership in schools with robust communities and those with weak communities (Youngs & King, 2002): "[P]rincipals can construct their role to either support or inhibit the strength and quality of teacher community" (McLaughlin & Talbert, 2001, p. 101). More and more, we are discovering that it is the principal who acts as the catalyst to bring other important supports to life (Bryk et al., 2010; Murphy, 2013a). Without effective leadership, resources, time, and structures have almost no hope of emerging to support collaborative work (Cosner, 2009; Hayes et al., 2004). We also know that principal leadership and professional community are interdependent, having an iterative relationship (McLaughlin & Talbert, 2001). Perhaps most importantly, there is a growing knowledge base that suggests that of all the ways that principals have at their disposal to influence teacher learning, developing and supporting collaborative communities of professional practice may be the most powerful (Supovitz et al., 2010).

It is important to acknowledge that for many principals, growing community necessitates a difficult transformation of their own understanding of leadership and their own leadership roles (Goldstein, 2004; Murphy, 2005). "The implications for school principals are considerable" (Crowther, Kaagan, Ferguson, & Hann, 2002, p. 64), and this repositioning presents a real challenge for principals (Brown & Sheppard, 1999). Communities of practice are, in some essential ways, "at odds with the dominant conceptions of the principalship that have been in place in most educational systems for decades" (Crowther et al., 2002, p. 6). Thus, just as teachers are being asked to step outside traditional perspectives of their roles, so also must principals think in new ways about their roles (Harrison & Lembeck, 1996; Mayrowetz, Murphy, Seashore Louis, & Smylie, 2009; Murphy, 2005). Fostering the development of communities of practice necessitates a new knowledge and skill base and a new set of performances that are not often found in the education of school administrators (Blegen & Kennedy, 2000; Childs-Bowen, Moller, & Scrivner, 2000; Murphy, 2005). New metaphors for the principalship emerge as well—metaphors that reflect the role of the principal not in terms of one's fit in the organizational structure but in terms of membership in a community of learners (Beck & Murphy, 1992; Klecker & Loadman, 1998; Scribner et al., 1999; Sergiovanni, 1991a, 1991b).

The point to be underscored here is that for many principals, a personal transformation in leadership must accompany the quest to rebuild schooling to cultivate communities of practice. Absent this change, it is difficult to imagine that principals will develop a sense of security. Likewise, cultivating teacher community in a hierarchical and bureaucratic organizational seedbed is problematic at best (Murphy, 1991, 2013b). New conceptions of organizations provide the foundations for developing the skills to foster norms of community (Murphy, 2002). This is challenging work, but principals who do not begin here are not likely to be effective in making teacher inquiry a reality in their schools.

Frameworks of Support

Over the years, analysts have cobbled together various frameworks to capture the array of factors and conditions that principals can use to support the development of teacher communities. Stoll and colleagues (2006, p. 23) employ four categories: focusing on learning processes, making the best of human and social resources, managing structural resources, and interacting with and drawing on external agents. Mullen and Hutinger (2008, p. 280) also describe four sets of leader actions: manage resources, provide support and direction, exert appropriate pressure to achieve goals, and mediate group dynamics. Printy (2008, p. 211) discusses three principal functions: communicate vision, support teachers, and buffer teachers from outside influences. McLaughlin and Talbert (2001) offer this list of related actions:

> For better or worse, principals set conditions for teacher community by the ways in which they manage school resources, relate to teachers and students, support or inhibit social interactions and leadership in the faculty, respond to the broader policy context, and bring resources into the school. (p. 98)

In their work, Supovitz and Poglinco (2001) uncovered five strategies that leaders employ in their efforts to create professional communities of practice:

> First, these instructional leaders carefully developed a safe environment within which their teachers could take the risks associated with change. Second, they emphasized open channels of communication and strong collaboration amongst their faculty for the purpose of expanding the networks of engagement around issues of instructional improvement. Third, they cultivated informal and formal leaders in their schools to both allow themselves time for instructional attention and to broaden the base for change in the school. Fourth, [they] employed powerful and symbolic actions and events to dramatize and reinforce their message. Finally, they developed strong systems for accountability even as they expanded teachers' flexibility to further develop their instructional practices. (p. 7)

A slightly different architecture is provided by Printy (2008) who sees community building occurring through three roles:

> As agenda setters, leaders select policy messages to communicate to teachers and establish specific expectations or goals for teachers' work. As knowledge brokers, leaders focus teachers' attention on instructional matters, create the conditions for productive teacher conversations, scaffold teachers' learning as appropriate, and

facilitate the translation and alignment of meanings across communities. As learning motivators, leaders nurture positive relationships, establish urgency for new approaches and hold teachers accountable for results, in essence tightening the connections between policy and practice. (p. 199)

Saunders and team (2009, p. 1028) highlight the centrality of time, administrative support, and structures—issues examined throughout this volume. This is consistent with our claim that the traditional function of principals can be engaged to nurture collaborative work (e.g., coordinating, monitoring). More parsimonious leadership frames have been provided by Kruse and associates (1995, p. 34), such as structural conditions and characteristics of human resources; by Hurd (cited in Morrissey, 2000, p. 6), such as structural conditions and collegial relationships; and by McDougall and colleagues (2007, p. 54), such as settings and processes. Taking a slightly different approach, Scribner and team (1999) describe administrative, moral, and political support from the principal employed in the service of creating communities of practice.

Starting with the groundwork presented above, we explore what the research confirms about the specific leader acts that foster professional communities. Before we do so, however, we need to reinforce some core ideas. First, the goal of leadership is not the development of learning communities. The objective is the creation of human and social capital that enhances the quality of instruction in the service of student learning. The wager here is that such communities provide a robust pathway to reach these more-distal ends. Second, the focus is not primarily on beefing up each element of communities of practice individually. The best strategy is to deploy supports that forge an integrated scaffolding.

Finally, there are two activities that receive very limited treatment in the educational literature but rise to the level of considerable importance in the research on organizations more broadly defined (Wenger & Snyder, 2000). To begin with, an essential responsibility of the principal is to identify people with the commitment, energy, and skills to do good work and bring them together, recognizing that these forged communities often do not follow existing organizational structures (e.g., grade level). Also important is the need for leaders to identify existing informal associations of people with shared interests (e.g., worries about a spike in the number of homeless children in the school) and support them in functioning as collaborative communities. A key insight from these two lessons is that community is not isomorphic with the organizational chart.

Activity Domains

As is the case throughout the book, we carefully and deliberately build on the work of colleagues to arrive at our framework of principal supports for teacher communities. Concomitantly, we add new pillars to the structure and contextualize and add nuance to the collective body of evidence. We examine the following supports—creating structures and time, supporting learning, and managing the work—all of which are integrated with earlier analyses.

Creating Structures and Time

We know a good deal about organizational structures in general and in the area of school improvement more specifically. As we reported earlier, structures shape what unfolds in schools, partially determining what is and what is not possible. On the flip side of culture, structures allow norms to flourish or wither (Brooks, Scribner, & Eferakorho, 2004; Kruse et al., 1995; Leithwood, Day, Sammons, Harris, & Hopkins, 2006). Our focus at this point in the analysis is on the positive side of the narrative— that is, how well-resourced and thoughtfully developed forums in schools can help collaborative communities grow. The door through which we enter the analysis is *collaboration*, the element of shared work that provides a seedbed for the growth of relationships, shared trust, and mutual responsibility (Bryk et al., 2010). In short, we review what is known about creating the supportive collaborative frame we detailed above.

A recurring theme throughout our work is that structural change does not predict organizational performance—student learning in the case of schools (Murphy, 1991, 2013a). We are also cognizant that simply giving teachers a platform to talk in will not ensure the development of valued professional norms and human and social capital (Levine & Marcus, 2007; Newmann et al., 2001). So while we acknowledge the essentiality of time and space to undertake collaborative work, we define structure in terms that underscore what is required for principals to power community. At the core then, structure is about "interactive settings" (Cosner, 2009, p. 255) and "interaction patterns" (p. 273). It is about opportunities for forging relationships, for creating patterns of networks, and for promoting professional exchange through new channels of communication (May & Supovitz, 2011; Stoll et al., 2006). In short, it is about fostering professional collaboration (Ancess, 2003; Cosner, 2009).

Research helps us discern some ways principals work structurally to create and nurture teacher communities. On the issue of forums, first, there is unanimous agreement that schools must take advantage of existing space and time configurations, to repurpose them (Cosner, 2009; Stein & Coburn, 2008). For example, community-building work is conspicuous by its absence from most faculty meetings. Principals can repurpose these and many other meetings to deepen collaboration. At the same time, as we detail below, there is general agreement that new forums will need to be created as well (Ermeling, 2010). Third, a variety of community-building structures are needed, not simply reliance on professional learning community meetings (Leithwood et al., 2006; McLaughlin & Talbert, 2001).

Analysts also advance the idea that both formal and informal opportunities for building community need to be realized, with an eye open especially for the informal opportunities that often lay fallow (Cosner, 2009; McLaughlin & Talbert, 2001). As we discussed above, joining together teachers who—in informal ways—already demonstrate working connections, beliefs, and relationships can be an important piece of a principal's community building plan (Penuel et al., 2009; Useem et al., 1997). Additionally, Raywid (1995) reminds us of the importance of nurturing the relationships among individual teachers in the service of community development.

Lastly, it appears that creating structures that promote both horizontal and vertical networks and exchanges is wise (Johnson & Asera, 1999). Here, scholars point to collaborative structures that stimulate cross-grade and cross-departmental linkages, what Cosner (2009) calls "new interaction patterns" (pp. 268–269). Also emphasized here are forums that allow teachers from different collective teams to collaborate (Kruse et al., 1995; Stein & Coburn, 2008) by "structuring communities with overlapping boundaries and multimembership" (Printy, 2008, p. 217).

The handmaiden to structure is time (Harris, 2003; York-Barr & Duke, 2004). Without time, the development of collaborative forums becomes nearly impossible (Darling-Hammond & McLaughlin, 1995; Eilers & Camacho, 2007). Alternatively, teacher community researchers reveal that in schools, community flourishes when leaders make time available for collaborative work and professional learning (Huberman et al., 2011; Youngs, 2007). A similar conclusion is evident in studies of effective schools in general (Blase & Blase, 2004; Drago-Severson, 2004).

Researchers have also teased out clues about how principals can employ space and time in the service of community development. One approach to enhance interactions is to bring members of current or proposed collaboratives into close physical proximity (Bulkley & Hicks, 2004; Supovitz, 2008). According to these investigators, proximity can assist in overcoming dysfunctional norms such as privatization and egalitarianism (Gray et al., 1999; Kruse et al., 1995). A second suggestion is to take maximum advantage of formal teacher leadership positions in schools (e.g., data coach) and have them organize and lead forums in which small groups of teachers can interact (Cosner, 2009; Murphy, 2005). Relatedly, collaboration can be nurtured by infusing integrated leadership throughout the school (Leithwood et al., 2006; Silins & Mulford, 2004). Lastly, leaders moving to deepen collaborative communities of professional practice can create what Saunders and team (2009, p. 1011) call "predictable, consistent settings;" what Blase and Blase (2004, p. 68) refer to as "teacher collaborative structures;" and what Ermeling (2010, p. 387) describes as "dedicated and protected times where teachers meet on a regular basis to get important work done." As posited above, these can be new arrangements or repurposed existing settings. Whatever the designs, these predictable, patterned forums are the most efficacious method principals have of enhancing community development among teachers (Pounder, 1999).

Our review also uncovers information on specific forums principals can put in play to foster stronger collaboration (Penuel et al., 2009). Repurposed staff and departmental meetings find a home here, as do reconfigured school schedules to allow for late start or early dismissal on selected days (Cosner, 2009; King, 2001; Mitchell & Castle, 2005; Spillane et al., 2001). Creating blocks of time for teachers to observe in a classroom of peers is a special category of collaboration (Blase & Blase, 2004; Harris, 2003). Ad hoc groups such as book study teams, inquiry groups, and action research teams are found in some community-anchored schools, as are structures and time for teachers to collaborate around school governance and planning (Cosner, 2009; Leithwood et al., 2006; McLaughlin & Talbert, 2001; Newmann et al., 2001). Induction and mentoring programs can provide forums to stimulate collaboration and learning as well as the use of team teaching arrangements (Johnson & Asera, 1999; Kruse et al., 1995; Youngs, 2007). The strategy most often employed by leaders is the creation of a master schedule that establishes common planning time for groups of teachers, usually by grade level, subject area, or teaching team (Cosner, 2009).

Finally, a cross-cutting analysis of the research on teacher communities exposes some of the essential touchstones of these collaborative forums. We learn that these gatherings for work and learning should (1) occur frequently, for a reasonable block of time, and across the full year; (2) be intensive; (3) focus on student learning and instructional matters; (4) maximize interdependency; and (5) feature specific tasks that structure time usage (Center for Teaching Quality, 2007; Cosner, 2009; Felner et al., 2007; Hiebert & Pearson, 1999; Johnson & Asera, 1999; Kruse et al., 1995; Murphy, 2005; Penuel et al., 2009; Raywid, 1995). We also know that resources such as protocols are often associated with productive use of collaborative time.

Supporting Learning

Time and working structures are important and necessary. But they are insufficient to power communities of practice (Ancess, 2003; Ermeling, 2010). As we have noted above, teacher communities produce valued outcomes by fostering the development of professional norms and promoting teacher learning. Leaving this to happen by chance is not a wise idea. What is required is what we call *learning to learn*, the development of the knowledge and the mastery of skills that make teacher growth a reality, what Supovitz (2002) refers to as "continuous capacity building" (p. 1618). We examine the work of the principal in activating the *learning* in the *learning to learn* paradigm for learning communities below.

For most teachers, working with students is a nearly all-consuming activity. Consequently, they have spent very little time working with other adults. Not surprisingly, therefore, having principals work with teachers to develop "managerial skills in dealing with people" (Ainscow & Southworth, 1996, p. 234) is an essential component of professional development designed to help teachers work effectively in learning communities (Adams, 2010; Borko, 2004). Or, as Little (1987) captures it, "the specific skills and perspectives of working with a colleague are critical" (p. 512) for teacher communities to develop. The centrality of building relationships cannot be overstated in the work of practice communities, neither can the development of relationship-building capabilities (Cosner, 2009; Lynch & Strodl, 1991) or the role of the principal in making this happen.

Scholars have isolated an assortment of interpersonal capacities that principals can help nurture to promote productive working relationships among teachers (Brooks et al., 2004). They conclude that professional development should assist teachers in developing proficiencies around a number of interpersonal issues (Crow & Pounder, 2000). For example, Katzenmeyer and Moller (2001) conclude that development should begin with personal knowledge. Professional development in this area builds from the assumption that focusing "on increasing their own self-awareness, identify formation, and interpretive capacity" (Zimpher, 1988, p. 57) is critical. It is this understanding that permits teachers to (1) recognize the values, behaviors, philosophies, and professional concerns that underlie their personal performance and (2) understand their colleagues, especially those whose experiences and viewpoints do not mirror their own (Katzenmeyer & Moller, 2001).

A bushel of competencies that lubricate effective working relations are often mentioned as candidates for inclusion in professional development for teacher groups. For example, analysts assert that "skills that will make teachers sensitive to seeing others' points of view" (Katzenmeyer & Moller, 2001, p. 67) and "sensitive to others' needs" (LeBlanc & Shelton, 1997, p. 38) are important. Also, because teachers often "report that they became more influential through using good listening techniques with peers" (Katzenmeyer & Moller, 2001, p. 93), helping teachers increase proficiency in the area of listening skills is important. In a similar view, because the friction that sometimes surfaces in group interactions is greatly influenced by the form of those exchanges, communities are advantaged when teachers possess well-developed facilitation skills (Zimpher, 1988). In its broadest form, *facilitation* means "knowing how to help a group take primary responsibility for solving its problems and mitigat[ing] factors that hinder the group's ability to be effective" (Killion, 1996, p. 72). More specifically, it includes the ability to establish trust and rapport and to navigate through problems (Kilcher, 1992). Likewise, there is agreement that leaders need to arrange opportunities for teachers to develop consulting skills and proficiency in conferencing with colleagues if they are to be effective in inquiry communities (Manthei, 1992; Zimpher, 1988). The "principles and skills of advising" (Little, 1985, p. 34) are also key pieces in the portfolio of tools that help establish a productive context for collaborative work, as are influencing skills (Hart, 1995; Katzenmeyer & Moller, 2001).

In addition to the social lubrication skills just outlined, analysts assert that principals should arrange professional development activities that address a variety of skills for attacking joint work endeavors and provide a set of group process skills for understanding and managing the group dynamics that accompany collaborative work (Kilcher, 1992; Murphy, 2005). Perhaps most important here is the broad array of communication skills needed to interact with colleagues (LeBlanc & Shelton, 1997). Indeed, it is almost an article of faith in the literature in this area that inquiry communities "benefit from ongoing learning and practice in effective communication" (Killion, 1996, p. 72). Problem-solving and decision-making skills are also seen as quite important. As Killion (1996) reports, "[K]nowing various decision-making methods, selecting the most appropriate method for a particular situation, and having a repertoire of strategies for helping others reach a decision with the chosen methods are [also] critical skills" (p. 74). Finally, principals can help teachers benefit from community by ensuring that they master conflict management and conflict resolution skills (Fay, 1992; Hart, 1995). "Teacher[s] who not only understand the factors that lead to conflict but also have a range of strategies for managing and resolving it will be more successful" (Killion, 1996, p. 73) in communities of practice.

Managing the Work

The general message is that principals have two roles in the domain of managing collaboration. First, they need to get professional communities up and running. Second, they need to hold at bay the natural entropy associated with collaborative work. They must help keep communities viable and vibrant. They also need to master the craft of layering in multiple, integrated supports (Murphy & Torre, 2014).

Principals need to be diligent in setting expectations for communities of practice. A clear vision for inquiry communities must be crafted along with a tangible set of expectations (Murphy, 2005). Also, because prospects for community will be heavily influenced by school practices, values, and expectations, principals need to bolster community by crafting "enabling policies" (Lieberman & Miller, 1999, p. 28). Bishop, Tinley, and Berman (1997) outline the case as follows:

> Since policies usually guide the course of action of an organization, and their statements include objectives that guide the actions of a substantial portion of the total organization, teachers will believe that they are empowered when they feel that their actions are undergirded and protected by such formalized policy statements. (p. 78)

Little (1987) concurs, arguing that "at its strongest—most durable, most rigorously connected to problems of student learning, most commanding of teachers' energies, talents, and loyalties—cooperative work is a matter of school policy" (p. 512) and that "high levels of joint action are more likely to persist" (p. 508) when a supportive policy structure is in place.

As we documented earlier, throughout the research on implementation, change, and school improvement, the importance of adequate resources is a recurring theme. Nowhere is this finding more accurate than in the area of teacher communities (Mitchell & Sackney, 2006; Mullen & Hutinger, 2008). Resources (in addition to time) in the professional community research include materials such as "teachers' guides, activity sheets, and commercially prepared videos" (Burch & Spillane, 2003, p. 530). Protocols that direct collaborative work into productive channels is a type of material often underscored in studies of effective teacher communities (Cosner, 2011; Saunders et al., 2009). These designed activities help generate shared language, maintain focus, teach group process skills, and reinforce professional norms while damping down the dysfunctional behavior and project derailment often observed in work teams (Cosner, 2011; Young, 2006).

For teacher communities to function effectively, principals need to become active and central figures in communication systems, using both formal and informal procedures (Brooks et al., 2004; Walker & Slear, 2011). When this happens, understanding is deepened and questions and misconceptions are addressed before they can become toxic (Cosner, 2011; Kochanek, 2005).

Other community management responsibilities for principals can be teased out of the research as well. Not surprisingly, given its importance in the general literature, the principal has a central role in ensuring that explicit understandings of the rationale for, workings of, and outcomes needed from teacher communities are established (Printy, 2008; Quint, 2006). Analysts also affirm that principals in schools with well-functioning teacher communities are adept at buffering teachers from external pressures that can hinder progress (King, 2001; Rossmiller, 1992). They filter demands that are not aligned with community work and reshape others so that they do fit (Cosner, 2011; Printy, 2008; Robinson, 2007).

The necessity for leaders to be engaged in ongoing monitoring of the activities and outcomes of collaborative work is routinely discussed in the research as well (Quint, 2006; Stoll et al., 2006). Participation in community meetings, review of group documents, and comparative benchmarking are often featured in the monitoring portfolio (Heller & Firestone, 1995; Mullen & Hutinger, 2008). Monitoring that keeps "leaders in touch with teacher's ongoing thinking and development" (Levine & Marcus, 2007, p. 134) leads directly to another responsibility, that of providing feedback to collaborative work teams. A school culture that honors shared engagement is yet another indispensable element in the managing collaboration portfolio

(Harrison & Lembeck, 1996). So, too, is a system of incentives and rewards that mutually motivates teachers to privilege (Murphy, 2005). Currently, the picture that emerges from the literature is one in which there are few external incentives for community work. In fact, there are numerous disincentives to change to collaborative work at the heart of teacher communities (Little, 1988). In many schools, there is limited recognition for the work, and there are few rewards for additional effort (Crowther et al., 2002). In too many places, "the only rewards for teacher leadership are added responsibilities" (Moller & Katzenmeyer, 1996, p. 14).

In schools, two types of recognition are employed by principals to energize community building. First, since the actions of persons of status and influence carry considerable weight, they consciously work in this domain (Hart, 1994). Administrators, union leaders, and well-respected veteran teachers merit notice (Silins & Mulford, 2004). Second, principals ensure that the peer acceptance and recognition that is important to teachers—the absence of which can negatively affect the growth of teacher community in a school—is forthcoming (LeBlanc & Shelton, 1997; Mulford & Silins, 2003).

While "rewarding teachers who are willing to move beyond their classrooms to lead is a complicated issue" (Moller & Katzenmeyer, 1996, p. 13), in the end, principals "must provide incentives and rewards for teachers who take the lead in tackling tasks and solving problems" (Boles & Troen, 1996, p. 60): Leaders need to identify ways to acknowledge teachers in ways teachers value (Harrison & Lembeck, 1996). Moller and Katzenmeyer (1996) uncovered three ways in which principals were able to provide support and incentives for teacher work in communities of practice:

> First, the principals provided access to information and resources and gave their personal time. Second, they honored teacher leaders' request for professional development and sometimes initiated opportunities for them to attend conferences or represent the school at important meetings. Finally, they gave them the gift of time, covering classes for them, providing substitute teachers, or assigning support personnel to assist them. (pp. 13–14)

Responsibility for showcasing and providing recognition for quality work rests squarely with the principal (Drago-Severson, 2004; Mulford & Silins, 2003).

CONSEQUENCES

Throughout this chapter, we have introduced caveats into the analysis. As we turn now to the impact of professional development, we add to that list of cautions by focusing here on the firmness of knowledge around the consequences of teacher learning. We commence with the fact that the literature on the effects of professional development routinely features theoretical expectations about outcomes—what, given a supposed chain of logic, *should* happen. Second, measures of effects are often based on the perceptions of the people in whom change is expected. Direct observation of change is much less visible in the research. Third, the line of reasoning that creates "a chain of evidence that links student learning [backwards] to teaching learning, professional development, and policy is remarkably challenging" (Penuel et al., 2007, p. 953). As a result, there is considerably more evidence in the beginning links of the chain (e.g., change in teacher knowledge) than at the end of the chain (e.g., student learning). Finally, studies that are able to follow the full length of the logic chain from professional development experiences to student learning note more robust effects for earlier than later links (Hattie, 2009).

With these caveats in hand, there are still valuable insights about consequences that are woven in throughout the research. We learn from scholars employing varied lenses that quality professional development can have a strong and positive influence on teacher knowledge (Hattie, 2009; Penuel et al., 2007). Well-crafted and enacted professional learning also impacts teacher attitudes. For example, researchers document impacts on teacher motivation; self-esteem; commitment to the school, fellow teachers, and one's students; and individual and collective efficacy (Blase & Blase, 2000; Dannetta, 2002; Garet et al., 2001; Hawley & Valli, 1999; Leithwood et al., 2011). Keeping in mind the caveat about measuring impacts, we also know that quality professional development promotes changes in teachers' practice in classrooms (Desimone et al., 2002; Hamilton et al., 2003). It also ramps up "innovation/creativity, variety in teaching and risk taking" (Blase & Blase, 2000, p. 136).

Moving to the impact of professional development on schools, there is evidence that quality learning helps principals along the same chain of logic as for teachers—in knowledge, attitudes, and practice (Burch & Spillane, 2003; Robinson, 2007). In a reciprocal fashion, it often strengthens professional community (McLaughlin & Talbert, 2001). Professional development has been linked to improved school capacity, increases in academic press, and increased teacher retention (Bryk et al., 2010; Leithwood et al., 2011; Newmann et al., 2000; Youngs, 2007).

Finally, quality professional development impacts students. We learn that effective professional development that includes productive feedback has a moderate influence on student learning (Borko, 2004; Bryk et al., 2010; Caldwell, 1998; Hattie, 2009; Hawley & Valli, 1999).

In Part IV of the book, we turn from instructional capacity in schools to the academic norms of effective schools (Chapter 7) and the instructional practices in classrooms where all children reach ambitious learning goals (Chapter 8).

PART IV

Leading the Curricular Program

7

School as Academic Place

In the last two chapters, we used our broadest lens to explore instructional capacity and the avenues available to leaders to build high-capacity schools. In this chapter, we employ a mid-sized prism to investigate how leaders can help create a climate of instructional press in schools. The focus is on forging and nurturing broad norms of schools as academic places. We find that norms give meaning to pedagogical work in classrooms, and pedagogical actions help define norms of schools as academic places. Collectively, instructional capacity, norms of the school as an academic place, and effective instructional programs help foster academic press.

We begin with some reminders. While the focus of this volume is on academic press, all great schools rest on two pillars: school as academic place and supportive community. Rossmiller (1992) described these as technical competence and human relationship; Hayes and associates (2004) stated that "[p]roductive pedagogies are intellectually challenging and embedded within a highly supportive classroom" (p. 520).

Alone and intertwined with supportive community, school as academic place has a significant impact on student achievement (Leithwood, Patten, & Jantzi, 2010; Rutter, 1983). That effect, in turn, is mediated by student engagement, which itself is shaped directly by enhanced student motivation and commitment. What makes this mediated chain so important is that student engagement in school is considerably lower than teachers believe. According to Csikszentmihalyi and Larson (1984) and Yair (2000), the average student engagement rate is around 50 percent: "The average student pays little attention to the goals of the classroom and does so without enthusiasm or pleasure" (Csikszentmihalyi & Larson, 1984, p. 207). He or she "is usually bored, apathetic, and unfriendly to the situation" (p. 205). Engagement is lowest during the most heavily emphasized instructional formats in schools: teacher-centered instruction. In those contexts, it is lower still for students of color (Yair, 2000). Disengagement also increases as youngsters move up through the grades (Collins & Valentine, 2010; Yair, 2000).

The essential message for creating schools as academic places is that because it is "inconceivable that major improvements in student learning can occur without fundamental changes in the way students interact with teachers around subject matter" (Bryk, Sebring, Allensworth, Luppescu, & Easton, 2010, p. 47), we need to change the places in which students find themselves (Farrell, 1990). Strategies to "interrupt the process of disidentification" (Voelkl, 1997, p. 294) must be the highest priority for teachers and school leaders. This, of course, exposes the central problem of boredom in schools. It also leads to this inescapable conclusion:

> Current school organizational and instructional practices produce high rates of student disengagement, undercutting the possible contribution of time as a viable resource. Indeed, variation in student engagement, accounted for by variation of instruction characteristics, suggests that instructional reform may be a potent vehicle in affecting student outcomes. (Yair, 2000, p. 504)

We turn now to the norms that define a school as an academic place: academic care, challenge, task-focused goals, active learning, engagement and vitality, cooperative learning, meaningfulness, student-anchored learning, and evidence-based decision making and feedback.

ACADEMIC CARE

Across the landscape of work on productive classrooms and effective schools, we find that educators employ caring relationships with students to foster the development of powerful academic norms (Marks, 2000; Murphy & Torre, 2014). Ancess (2003, p. 80) captures this point when she reminds us that "relationships are a pedagogical tool," that teachers harness relationships in the service of academic achievement. Her research also reinforces the conclusion that the "most effective pedagogical tool is the capability of knowing students well" (p. 84). According to Wilson and Corbett (1999), students describe good teachers as those who care about them and make them learn. They often describe caring student-teacher relationships as academic in nature (Antrop-Gonzalez, 2006; Scanlan & Lopez, 2012). Academic care becomes a blend of personalized support and press for academic mastery (Alder, 2002; Kleinfeld, 1975).

Students explain the norm of academic care in a variety of ways. They describe teachers who do not let them fall through the cracks or become invisible (Patterson, Beltyukova, Berman, & Francis, 2007). They discuss teachers who push and pull them to understanding and success (Patterson et al., 2007; Wilson & Corcoran, 1988). In places where the norms of academic care flourish, teachers cajole, nudge, and command students to complete assignments. They are alert, approachable, and helpful (Ancess, 2003; Wilson & Corcoran, 1988). They build safety nets to ensure success (Smerdon, Borman, & Hannaway, 2009), "enabling webs of support" (Cooper, Ponder, Merritt, & Matthews, 2005, p. 20). Teachers ensure that every child receives the academic support he or she needs (Wilson & Corcoran, 1988). "They intervene to prevent failure" (Cooper et al., 2005, p. 10), employing a variety of academic care strategies to ensure this outcome (Quint, 2006; Rumberger, 2011). Academic care is about a combination of safe work environments, where disruptions do not undercut student efforts (Sebastian & Allensworth, 2012) and where students "feel safe to learn, re-learn, and explore knowledge and understanding" (Hattie, 2009, p. 239).

CHALLENGE

Effective classrooms and schools are characterized by academic challenge (Bryk et al., 2000; Hattie, 2009). They are "academically demanding" (Noguera, 1996, p. 232) places where there is "greater emphasis on mastering challenging content" (Wilson & Corbett, 1999, p. 92). Evidence from an assortment of studies and reviews affirms the centrality of the norm of challenge in the learning narrative and its influence on "multiple consequences" of interest (Hattie, 2009, p. 246). Csikszentmihalyi and Larson's (1984) research shows how students unplug during unchallenging work experiences. Barnett and colleagues (2001), for example, conclude that "students are likely to resist learned helplessness, try harder, and persist longer when faced with a challenging and difficult task" (p. 28). In his seminal meta-analysis, Hattie (2009) reports larger effect sizes on student engagement for challenging than for moderately challenging instruction. Yair (2000) documents similar effects, reporting that "the odds of students engaging in their lessons in what they named 'most challenging' are 90% higher than the odds in the lessons students identify as 'least challenging'" (p. 501). The conclusion is clear: When "students report challenge, they also report engagement" (Yair, 2000, p. 501). "Students are most engaged by instruction that is cognitively challenging" (Marks, 2000,

p. 159). Collins and Valentine (2010) find powerful effects for challenge on learning outcomes. And when we substitute *expectations* for *challenge*, we arrive at the same end point (Hattie, 2009). That is, "the higher a teacher's expectations for a student, the higher the student's achievement" (Hallinan & Kubitschek, 1999, p. 46).

Unfortunately, as is the case for all of the norms of academic place, challenge is often underdeveloped in schools. As we have seen repeatedly throughout the book, engagement is often conspicuous by its absence in schools. We add here that some part of this lack of engagement is traceable to a lack of challenge in classrooms, especially in terms of expectations and assignments (Drago-Severson, 2004; Quint, 2006; Yair, 2000). We confirm also that schools and classrooms often reinforce rather than disrupt the expectations and demands students carry with them from interactions in other societal institutions (Eckert, 1989; Hattie, 2009).

Researchers also convey the importance of context and nuance around the norm of challenge. To begin with, it is not a fixed quality. It can only be understood in reference to students (Hattie, 2009) and "in relation to the actor's skills" (Csikszentmihalyi & Larson, 1984, p. 251). Thus, by definition, challenge is always a moving target, increasing as the skills and knowledge of the learners are strengthened. Therefore, the critical issue is "challenging students at the appropriate level" (Hattie, 2009, p. 99), "where knowledge can be mastered when the student really tries hard" (Csikszentmihalyi & Larson, 1984, p. 266).

While it is not our goal in this chapter to discuss specific pedagogical moves, the research does afford some insights about how schools can bring challenge to life. Some of these are curricular in nature and are discussed in Chapter 8. Here, we see moves such as increasing rigor, ratcheting up curricular expectations, increasing the amount of meaningful work to be completed, and providing scaffolding to help students reach course objectives. The essential caveat here is that the answers are found not in the structures and policies that are imported (e.g., block scheduling, team teaching) but the norms of the school as academic place. In short, while structure and polices do not predict outcomes, norms do (Elmore, 1995; Murphy, 1991, 2013a; Murphy & Torre, 2014).

On the instructional side of the ledger, at the broad level, we find the provision of "more stimulating and academically rigorous instruction [as well as] instruction that emphasizes critical thinking and problem solving" (Carbonaro & Gamoran, 2002, p. 803). Also found here are teachers who "establish challenging standards for student performance, cover content in ways that promote student understanding and desire to learn more, and regularly assign meaningful homework" (Shouse, 1996, p. 50), teachers who push youngsters further in their thinking (Brewer, 1993; Darling-Hammond, Ancess, & Ort, 2002). They correct mistakes and provide abundant feedback (Gamoran, 1996; Hattie, 2009).

TASK-FOCUSED GOALS

Scholars over the last 30 years have uncovered the significance of a specific dimension of challenge—goals—to the development of classrooms and schools as academic places (Scanlan & Lopez, 2012). According to Hattie (2009), "[S]etting challenging goals is a powerful part of the overall equation of what makes the difference in learning" (p. 199). Of particular interest here is the difference in emphasis on task-oriented goals (also known as *mastery goals*) versus performance-oriented goals. Task-oriented goals address establishing expectations to achievement targets. Performance-oriented goals focus on comparisons of student learning outcomes (Barnett et al., 2001; Hattie, 2009). Task-oriented goals underscore effort. Performance-oriented goals underscore ability (Barnett et al., 2001).

Task-oriented goals have been shown to be an important dimension of school as academic place. We know, for example, that classrooms with task or learning-focused goals are more apt to "use 'deep' processing strategies such as relating newly learned material with previously learned material and to try to understand conceptual and abstract relationships" (Barnett et al., 2001, p. 28).

Task-oriented goals are characterized by clarity in the specifics of the learning intentions (i.e., they provide directional guidance to staff and students) and difficulty and specificity (Hattie, 2009). As was the case with challenge in general, challenging goals work best when they exist in the company of the other norms (e.g., cooperative work) of the school as academic place. For example, challenging goals work best when they are coupled with varied and meaningful learning opportunities, feature "tasks that are structured so that participants can attain the goals" (Hattie, 2009, p. 294), provide large doses of feedback from teachers (and peers), make success clear and visible in comparison to mastery rather than in comparison to the performance of other children, underscore problem-anchored activities, and highlight collaborative efforts.

As is the case with each of the norms of academic place, we know that task-focused goals lead to important outcomes. They promote greater effort on the part of students and deep persistence with assignments, ramp up engagement, and increase student learning (Hattie, 2009; Shouse, 1996). For example, in his cardinal analysis, Hattie (2009) concludes that "the performance of students who have the most challenging goals is over 250 percent higher than the performance of the subjects with easiest goals" (p. 164).

ACTIVE LEARNING

Over the course of this volume, we have reported that (1) teachers occupy center stage in classes for the overwhelming bulk of the day, something in the neighborhood of 80 percent of time; (2) lecture and discussion is the disproportionately preferred method of teaching; (3) about one third of the time, teachers are teaching what students already know; and (4) students are engaged in their classes no more than 50 percent of available class time on average. For a not-insignificant part of the school day, teachers and students are involved in the learning process in only a ritualistic fashion (Weis, 1990). The sequela is hardly surprising: Neither extrinsic nor intrinsic motivation develops. Effort is withheld. Students learn considerably less than they are capable of and less than what would be helpful to them to be successful in school and beyond.

Schools as academic places, on the other hand, are characterized as venues of active learning (McLaughlin & Talbert, 2001). Unlike traditional schools, they privilege learning over teaching. The focus is less about the transmission of knowledge and more about the construction of understanding (Prawat & Peterson, 1999). It is less about individualism and more about collaboration. According to Hattie (2009), under the norm of active learning, "learning is the explicit goal and there are active, passionate, and engaging people (teachers, students, peers, and so on) participating in the act of learning" (p. 22). The framework of school as academic place is about "engaging youth in their own learning" (Joselowsky, 2007, p. 268). In active learning, teachers are unquestionably authoritative directors of action, not merely facilitators, but not authoritarian (Hattie, 2009). They are less about telling and presenting academic work than requiring children to be active initiators of their own learning under the guidance of academically caring adults (Prawat & Peterson, 1999). Teachers construct "highly structured activities in which [youngsters] can use their skills within an organized framework" (Csikszentmihalyi & Larson, 1984, p. 95). In short, as Hattie (2009) describes, academic places are defined by "very active, direct involvement, and [a] high sense of agency" (p. 233).

Given the reality that "only by securing students' active involvement with instruction can time agendas have an effect" (Yair, 2000, p. 504), we should not be surprised to learn that active learning has been consistently found to be linked to student autonomy, self-regulation, and achievement (Hattie, 2009). And as we reported with the other norms, active learning works best in the portfolio of norms of academic place than as a singular characteristic (Bryk et al., 2010). It is associated with enhanced student sensemaking, commitment, and understanding (Ancess, 2003).

ENGAGEMENT AND VITALITY

Schools as academic places are venues of participation and engagement, not passivity, ritual, and boredom (Sebastian & Allensworth, 2012; Strahan, 2003). "Students' active participation in class is the main cause of their perception of high engagement rates" (Yair, 2000, p. 498). And, in turn, "engaging instructional tasks within a well-organized curriculum is an essential basis for improving student learning" (Bryk et al., 2010, p. 121).

Researchers and practitioners provide useful details in the narrative on student engagement. We know from the discussion above that school as academic place is both student centered and teacher directed. Students in engaging classrooms have voice and choice (Ancess, 2003). They are in places where construction trumps transmission. Thus, the norm of engagement underscores project-based learning opportunities and application-oriented tasks as well as work that is interesting, varied, and meaningful (Bryk et al., 2010; Cotton, 2000; Csikszentmihalyi & Larson, 1984; Hattie, 2009). In engaging classrooms (or when the norm of engagement and vitality is present) one is likely to find cooperative and student-directed learning experiences (Baker, Terry, Briger, & Winsor, 1997). In schools as academic places, teachers "ask more questions, elicit more critical thinking and student discussion, . . . [and] use problem-solving approaches to address student-initiated questions" (p. 59).

As we have reported on each of the other norms of schools as academic places, measurable benefits flow to schools from the norm of engagement and vitality, benefits such as improved attitudes toward subject domains, augmentation in critical thinking skills, positive affect, and enhanced achievement (Hattie, 2009). Engagement in school as academic place is described by Csikszentmihalyi and Larson (1984) as "flow, . . . a state of deep involvement in which the clock is figuratively turned off, where there is a loss of consciousness" (p. 250). That is, active, guided, engaged learning brings inspiration and vitality to school in general and to the teaching-learning process in particular (Farrell, 1990; Noguera, 1996). Academic place is about energy, excitement, and meaningfulness. Csikszentmihalyi and Larson (1984) go on to explain that traveling down the pathway of engagement and vitality

> would mean that educators might stop worrying about how to transmit information, and concentrate instead on how to make learning enjoyable, because only when going to school becomes a flow activity will students be motivated to learn on their own, and grow in the process. (p. 289)

COOPERATIVE LEARNING

We share a perhaps obvious but essential reminder: The norms of school as academic place are interlocking and share a good deal of space. The more of them that materialize in robust ways, the better things are for school improvement and student learning. So far, we have examined five of these norms: academic care, challenge, task-focused goals, active learning, and engagement and vitality. Here, we turn to the sixth norm, cooperative learning. This norm is also described in terms of *collaboration, inclusion,* and *integration* (Ancess, 2000; Woloszyk, 1996). McLaughlin and Talbert (2001) take us to the heart of the matter when they refer to the process of "establishing classroom environments in which students can learn as members of communities" (p. 134). Collaborative work challenges a number of underpinnings of traditional classrooms. It pushes back on the belief in imparted wisdom, the nearly exclusive centrality of the transmission of knowledge, what Eckert (1989) refers to as the *authoritarian aspects* of the classroom. It also underscores the importance of task completion, rolling back a primary focus on the competitive aspects of the classroom. Finally, we see that the academic norms of community-focused learning pushes from the center stage the notion that learning is predominantly an individual activity.

Collaborative learning requires that students attend to task-focused and challenging goals to accomplish meaningful work (Farrell, 1990). Ancess (2003) informs us that the essential element here is that "students are responsible for another's learning as well as their own" (p. 108). There is a palpable sense of interdependency in classrooms, a sense that "each person is benefiting from the work that the other kids are doing" (Ancess, 2003, p. 108). And as Farrell (1990) astutely reports, collaborative forms are only part of the storyline here: "The group unity depends on the work that is undertaken, on the nature of the activity" (p. 59).

The empirical scorecard on the value of the norm of collaboration is quite positive in general and particularly robust for groups of students who often do not flourish in schools, such as minority students and those from working-class families (Ancess, 2000, 2003; Eckert, 1989; Hattie, 2009). "[T]here seems to be a universal agreement that cooperative learning is effective, especially when contrasted with competitive and individualist learning" (Hattie, 2009, p. 212) and especially in terms of student achievement (Ancess, 2003).

Analysis of the school as academic place norm of collaboration spotlights the importance of the topic of peers in classrooms, with eyes focused directly on "creating opportunities for cooperative learning between students" (Joselowsky, 2007, p. 269) and for promoting peer co-teaching (Hattie, 2009). We enter the discussion with the reminders that students have a tremendous say about what they do or do not learn and that "peers in general provide rich opportunities for interaction" (Csikszentmihalyi & Larson, 1984, p. 165). We layer in the reality that peer work runs against the ingrained norms in learning and teaching, such as "learning is an individual pursuit," "competition is the appropriate framework for learning," and "learning occurs primarily through transmission." Not surprisingly, then, collaboration is not part of the fabric of most schools (Hattie, 2009).

We know that schools that promote the concept of academic place consciously work to shape peer culture in classrooms and at the school level (Baker et al., 1997). Researchers help us see that teachers bring the collaborative norm to life by using peers as co-teachers and peer tutors. They "encourage interactions among students" (Joselowsky, 2007, p. 269). Researchers also substantiate that engagement is an outcome of peer work and that learning benefits accrue in youngsters who work in a collaborative environment in general and in models of peer tutoring in particular, with a nod to cross-age over same-age tutoring (Hattie, 2009; Laffey, 1982).

MEANINGFULNESS

There is a considerable body of knowledge that reveals that schools as academic places are defined by meaningful work and authentic pedagogy (Baker et al., 1997; Marks, 2000). The norm of meaningfulness assumes a variety of forms in the literature, or more accurately, perhaps, is an amalgam of varied but highly related ideas. In its essence, it boils down to work in which youngsters are apt to become engaged (Baker et al., 1997; Rumberger, 2011). One dimension of this is the authenticity or decisiveness of the work, infusing activities with purpose and signaling that work is important (Csikszentmihalyi & Larson, 1984; Shouse, 1996). Meaningfulness also includes the element of *responsiveness*, the idea that schools and classrooms are adapted to the specific needs and interests of the students (Ancess, 2003; Scanlan & Lopez, 2012). The focus is on "interesting and relevant information" (Noguera, 1996, p. 231). The artificial barrier between school and the world outside of schooling is lowered (Eckert, 1989; Rumberger, 2011). As Csikszentmihalyi and Larson (1984) capture the norm, "[T]he activity of work [is] all of a piece with the rest of life" (p. 256). When the norm of meaningfulness is present, there is a heavy concentration on performance tasks and problem-based activities (Ancess, 2003; Darling-Hammond et al., 2002; Hattie, 2009). Multiple and varied ways exist for students to demonstrate understanding in ways that have value to students and to those outside the confines of the learning assignment (Farrell, 1990).

We also see in classes defined by the norm of meaningfulness that there is a strong strand of application of knowledge that supplements the development of knowledge (Hattie, 2009), what Bryk and colleagues (2010) refer to as "application-oriented instruction" (p. 209). Work is marked by concreteness as well as abstraction (Ancess, 2003). The significance of relevance is underscored here. Culturally relevant and culturally congruent activities are visible where the norm of meaningfulness is found (Jordan & Cooper, 2003). Here, we see instruction that "addresses the needs of all students, affirms students' cultural identity, and draws on students' background as an asset" (Scanlan & Lopez, 2012, p. 608). The essential idea is "cultural synchronization" (Jordan & Cooper, 2003, p. 205) or "culturally responsive teaching methods" (Scanlan & Lopez, 2012, p. 588). We also find a focus on work and outcomes valued by students and, consequently, on having students assume responsibility for their efforts (Ancess, 2003; Darling-Hammond et al., 2002; Laffey, 1982). When the norm of meaningfulness is present, group accountability and rewards supplement traditional, individual-based accountability (Hattie, 2009; Laffey, 1982). "Failure [as] a constant part of the school lives of many students" (Farrell, 1990, p. 87) is pushed aside in schools as academic places.

When, "from the students' perspective, instruction becomes interesting and has personal meaning, they are motivated to attend" (Bryk et al., 2010, p. 174). Meaningful instruction has a powerful pull on student engagement (Marks, 2000; Noguera, 1996). Indeed, as Yair (2000) concludes, "[T]he odds of students engaging in the classes they deem 'most relevant' are 108% higher than in the classes the students' dubbed the 'least relevant'" (p. 501). And, as we have shown, scholars consistently show that engagement is the gateway to learning (Murphy & Torre, 2014).

STUDENT-ANCHORED LEARNING

The eighth norm of school as academic place is student-anchored learning, a norm with a great deal of alignment with the earlier norms. At its core, it underscores students as powerful activists in their learning. At the macro level, this means educators are seeing schools and learning through the eyes of their students, not simply through the demands of the curriculum and the needs of the school as an institution (Farrell, 1990; Hattie, 2009; Murphy & Torre, 2014). It is about the "need to embrace students' priorities" (Ancess, 2003, p. 79). Some of the essential aspects of this norm have been woven into the narrative to this point in the chapter. We find here, for example, building instruction around the experiences of the learners, what Phillips (2003, p. 260) refers to as "contextualized instruction" and Ancess (2003, p. 111) calls "'need-to-know' instruction." We see this as making schools and schoolwork relevant to students (Quint, 2006; Yair, 2000), using "instructional activities that place an importance on students' lives and interests" (Scanlan & Lopez, 2012, p. 607), fitting classroom work to the larger world outside of schooling (Ancess, 2003; Farrell, 1990), and "emphasizing real-life applications" (Darling-Hammond et al., 2002, p. 660).

The norm of student-anchored work also includes teaching and learning in which student choice and voice receive considerable attention (Patterson et al., 2007; Rodríguez, 2008)—frames that are linked in turn to student commitment and engagement. As Bryk and team (2010) make clear, "we know that children are more engaged in schooling when they feel in control of their own learning" (p. 104). Yair (2000, p. 490) goes further, reporting that "educational researchers, psychologists, and sociologists agree that instruction will have positive effects on student learning if . . . it allows for student choice or autonomy," a conclusion confirmed by Carbonaro and Gamoran (2002).

Looking across the norms that define schools as academic places, we see the presence of three deeply entwined principles. First, these are places where "teaching [becomes] subordinated to learning" (Ancess, 2003, p. 109), where students are active parties of the school work and producers, not simply receivers, of learning. Second, "good classes" are defined primarily "on the basis of process rather than the content of teaching" (Farrell, 1990, p. 108). Third, these are places of academic community.

EVIDENCE-BASED DECISION MAKING AND FEEDBACK

Schools as academic places are distinguished by the attention given to evidence in decision-making processes (Hattie, 2009). There has been a great deal of attention devoted to data-based decision making over the last quarter century. This is appropriate. But we develop a deeper narrative here. Data-based decision making is often limited in important ways. It has generally been held that data are academic scores of one kind or another. More limiting still has been the restriction of data to standardized assessments. Most troubling has been the impoverished conceptions of monitoring and feedback in data-based decision making. A broader perspective highlights evidence for nearly all actions undertaken in schools and underscores the essential element of feedback.

In effective schools, evidence becomes a central plank in dialogue and decision making through the school and across the full spectrum of activities (Horn, 2010; Levine & Marcus, 2007). Schools as academic places are venues marked by a generalizable "narrative of inquiry" (Wilson & Berne, 1999, p. 200) and action on the academic and social learning of students (Ermeling, 2010; Hattie, 2009). In schools as academic places, considerable attention is devoted to the visible and explicit cause-effect connection between instructional decisions and student outcomes" (Ermeling, 2010, p. 379).

At the heart of evidence-based action is the principle of *feedback*. Hattie (2009) helps us see that there are three important aspects of feedback. The most familiar is feedback to students. He goes further, however, by reminding us that essential evidence results when "teachers pay attention to the formative effects of their teaching" (p. 181). The third area of evidence comes from students' self-assessment efforts (see also Stiggins & Chappuis, 2006). He establishes that the main purpose of feedback is to "reduce discrepancies between current understanding and performance and a learning intention or goal" (Hattie, 2009, p. 175). Hattie also lays out the key ingredients of helpful feedback: Productive feedback is focused on the level at which students are working. It is directed to progress on tasks and the processes embedded in those tasks rather than to the self at a personal level. It is generally positive in form; that is, "it provides information on correct rather than incorrect responses and it builds on changes from previous trials" (p. 175). Higher impact is found "when goals are specific and challenging but when task complexity is low" (p. 175).

8

Curriculum and Assessment

In the last chapter, we examined what is known about productive schooling by highlighting the norms of schools as academic places. We continue that work here by focusing the lens on the curricular and assessment dimensions of schooling, recognizing that how leaders manage these domains represents a critical aspect of how principals impact teaching and learning.

CURRICULUM

Before we move too deeply into curriculum, it is advisable to begin with some reminders and cautions. In this section, we will be talking about curriculum somewhat independently of the context in which it is nested. However, we need to remember that context is always important and that curriculum is tightly bound to the "structure, policies, and processes that are used to distribute learning opportunities in schools" (Cooper, 1996, p. 197). We also must remind ourselves that curriculum unfolds in specific cultures, cultures that can reinforce or damage the messages conveyed in the curriculum. We will also be examining each subdimension of curriculum by itself. However, in real schools, it is clear that these subdimensions are overlapping patterns in a larger tapestry. It is also true that this tapestry is itself a piece of a larger picture of the core technology of a school, sharing space and interacting with instruction and assessment. The three subdimensions of curriculum—rigor and opportunity to learn, authenticity and cultural relevance, and program coherence—are discussed in order below.

Rigor and Opportunity to Learn

Curriculum is the *what* of the instructional program, the content to which students are exposed. At a core level, it is useful to describe curriculum in terms of *quality* or rigor and *quantity* or content coverage (Carbonaro & Gamoran, 2002; Hallinan & Kubitschek, 1999). On the topic of quality, the spotlight is focused on the breadth and depth of content standards, concepts that are established by curricular frameworks and the scope and sequence of courses (Bryk, Sebring, Allensworth, Luppescu, & Easton, 2010; Conchas, 2001; Wilson & Corbett, 1999). In addition to inspecting the power of individual courses, it is also helpful to define *quality* in terms of the rigor of the sequences of courses available to students (Oakes & Guiton, 1995).

Building on the work of Brophy, Leithwood and colleagues (2004) outline the elements of a robust curriculum:

> This is a curriculum in which the instructional strategies, learning activities and assessment practices are clearly aligned and aimed at accomplishing the full array of knowledge, skills, attitudes and dispositions valued by society. The content of such a curriculum is organized in relation to a set of powerful ideas. Skills are taught with a view to their application in particular settings and for particular purposes. In addition, these skills include general learning and study skills, as well as skills specific to subject domains. (p. 62)

In a quality curriculum, "what is taught is worth knowing in the first place and is treated in sufficient depth to engage students' interests and offer them a challenge" (Cotton, 2000, p. 10). The touchstones are *meaningfulness* and *challenge*, what Louis and Marks (1998, p. 537) refer to as "intellectually serious work" and Carbonaro and Gamoran (2002, p. 819) label "intellectually challenging content." As we will see below, some patterns of coursework have considerably less rigor than others. We will also see that this "distribution of less" is charged with the dynamics of class, race, and ethnicity (Murphy & Hallinger, 1989).

On the *quantity* side of the curriculum ledger, the essential issue is content coverage or opportunity to learn (Murphy, 1988; Murphy & Hallinger, 1989). That is, quantity is determined by the overall amount of work students complete in individual courses and across their programs (i.e., sequence of courses) (Carbonaro & Gamoran, 2002). Quantity opportunities are defined not only by "credit accumulation" (Allensworth &

Easton, 2005, p. 16) but by a press to do more intellectually challenging work (Murphy, Weil, Hallinger, & Mitman, 1982; Shouse, 1996). Opportunity to learn also has a good deal to do with the pacing of content over individual classes, over time, and across schooling (Bryk et al., 2010; Goldenberg, 2004).

A combined narrative about curriculum quality and quantity is visible most clearly in analyses of curriculum differentiation, commonly known as *ability grouping and tracking*. The first thing we need to remember about tracking is that it is a direct proxy for opportunity to learn. On this point, we know that "[t]racking functions as a major source of unequal opportunities to learn" (Mickelson & Heath, 1999, p. 569).

The second acknowledgment to be made about tracking is that "track placements are strongly correlated with students' race and social class" (p. 567). The "assignment process . . . favors whites over blacks of equal ability" (Thompson & O'Quinn, 2001, p. 13) and affluent children over poor children of similar abilities (Miller, 1995). On this front, we know that these assignments have deep historical roots, beginning in the early 20th century with the inculcation of the social efficiency philosophy into education (Murphy, Beck, Crawford, & Hodges, 2001). Under this banner, schools became places in which youngsters were tapped and then educated to fill slots in the larger economy, a process decoupled from merit and laced with both classism and racism (Kliebard, 1995; Krug, 1964). Thus, "from the early beginnings of 'tracked' educational programs to contemporary schools, white and more affluent students have had opportunities and access to an education that differs markedly from the education provided for students of color and poverty" (Shannon & Bylsma, 2002, p. 29). Alternatively, "students of low-socioeconomic status are more likely to be placed in academic tracks less conducive to achievement" (Roscigno, 1998, p. 1035). Because of tracking, "serious inequalities in access to knowledge continue to exist in the nation's schools among students from different social classes and racial groups" (Miller, 1995, p. 233).

The third point to be made about tracking/ability grouping is that it is highly consequential (Lee & Burkam, 2003; Oakes, 1985). It "can reproduce or even exacerbate inequality" (Downey, von Hippel, & Broh, 2004, p. 165) and translate into low-income and "[b]lack student disadvantage" (Roscigno, 1999, p. 161). We concentrate our attention here on the link between tracking and learning outcomes. However, it is important to acknowledge that tracking is associated with other outcomes as well. For example, research informs us that track placements "affect students' self-concepts" (Irvine, 1990, p. 15) and self-esteem as well as exposure to "friendship networks" (Lucas & Gamoran, 2002, p. 175) in general and to motivated (or unmotivated) peers in particular (Alexander & McDill, 1976; Berends, Lucas, Sullivan, & Briggs, 2005; Cotton, 2000; Land & Legters, 2002).

Track assignments also shape an especially key variable in the student success story—"aspirations for the future" (Lucas & Gamoran, 2002, p. 175).

There is considerable evidence that track membership has marked consequences for the development of academic orientations and for aspirations for continued education, particularly for post-high school education plans (Alexander, Cook, & McDill, 1978; Oakes, 1985). Alexander and Cook (1982) and Heyns (1974) suggest that schools exercise their primary influence over pupil socioeconomic attainment through their role in helping students establish orientations toward educational goals. As Heyns (1974) notes, "[I]t is possible that schools play a more decisive role in the stratification system through encouraging and implementing aspirations than through altering patterns of achievement" (p. 1445). Work on the reproduction of cultural inequalities in American education through differential teaching of both the form and the "hidden curriculum" at different track levels and at schools with students of varying biosocial backgrounds lends support to this position. Since they cluster students of color, track placements and ability grouping have also been implicated in the resegregation of education, this time *within* schools, by race and class (Irvine, 1990; Rumberger & Palardy, 2005), what Mickelson and Heath (1999) call "second-generation segregation within schools" (p. 577). As such, it is held that "tracking policies and practices serve as the major vehicle to institutionalize and perpetuate racial divisions" (Cooper, 2000, p. 620) among school-aged youth and adults (Land & Legters, 2002).

Turning to student learning outcomes, research confirms that sorting students into curricular tracks is associated with high school graduation and degree completion in college (Camara & Schmidt, 1999; Lee & Burkam, 2003; Singham, 2003): "The academic rigor of the courses taken in middle school and high school not only affects students' current achievement, but also is the single most important predictor of college success" (Kober, 2001, p. 27). Studies also reveal the linkage between track assignment and measures of academic achievement (Alexander et al., 1978; Gamoran, 2000; Goodlad, 1984; Oakes, 1985; Roscigno, 1998; Strutchens & Silver, 2000; Tate, 1997; Weinstein, 1976). Overall then, "research shows that academic achievement is closely related to the rigor of the curriculum" (Barton, 2003, p. 8), that the rigor of the curriculum is tightly aligned to track placement (Miller, 1995; Murphy, Hallinger, & Lotto, 1986), and that "ability grouping, on average, has a negative effect on students on the lower tail of the distribution" (Roscigno, 1998, p. 1039).

Authenticity and Cultural Relevance

Authenticity in the domain of curriculum refers to the ability to match learning context to the ways in which students learn most effectively. It refers to curriculum that moves from abstract concepts to include tangible work. It carries meaning for students to learning activities. That is, authentic work is grounded not only in the standards but also in the values, goals, and interests of students (Noguera, 1996; Roney, Coleman, & Schlichting,

2007). Relevance is a core concept here, embedding learning in "contexts in which students are interested and [involving] topics about which they are curious" (Roney et al., 2007, p. 290). In short, curriculum is seen through the eyes of students as well as the eyes of the disciplines (Cook-Sather, 2006; Flutter & Rudduck, 2004; Rudduck, Chaplain, & Wallace, 1996, pp. 17–27). Considerable attention is devoted to "valid educational content" (Newmann, 1992, p. 206). Authentic work also has value and meaning beyond the instructional context. It includes "linking academic instruction to examples in students' everyday experiences" (Christle, Jolivette, & Nelson, 2005, p. 86). It features real-life problems, including those often emerging from young people themselves; a "broad curriculum base" (Day, 2005, p. 576); "active and inquiry-based learning" (Desimone, Porter, Garet, Yoon, & Birman, 2002, p. 87); project-based learning (Shear et al., 2008); and co-construction of products, including support from peers as well as teachers (Eggert, Thompson, Herting, & Nicholas, 1995; Farrell, 1990; Johnson & Asera, 1999).

Culturally relevant curriculum extends the notion of authenticity to the backgrounds of children, especially children (and families) that have been marginalized in the traditional curriculums in schools (Antrop-Gonzalez & De Jesus, 2006; Gault & Murphy, 1987; Shannon & Bylsma, 2002). More specifically, in many schools, "there often is a mismatch between curriculum and students' values" (Mukuria, 2002, p. 434). The curriculum often "devalues the home and experience" (Eckert, 1989, p. 10) of those from nonmainstream backgrounds (Quiroz, 2001). In short, in a culturally relevant curriculum, there is greater sensitivity to the assorted cultures at the school, in the community, and in the nation (Burns, Keyes, & Kusimo, 2005; Datnow, Borman, Stringfield, Overman, & Castellano, 2003; Murtadha, 2009; Scanlan & Lopez, 2012). This means, more concretely, that "the formal and informal curricula reflect the cultural values and political realities of the communities and provide students with educational and social experiences closely aligned with community and cultural resources" (Antrop-Gonzalez & De Jesus, 2006, p. 410).

Analysts who focus on culturally relevant curriculum have distilled a number of its defining elements. Such curriculum "bridges students' home lives with their school lives" (Scanlan & Lopez, 2012, p. 574). There is direct attention to "crossing racial and ethnic borders [and] integrating cultural, linguistic, and historical connections in the curriculum" (Galletta & Ayala, 2008, p. 1971). Culturally relevant curriculum "challenges the notion that assimilation is a neutral process" (Antrop-Gonzalez & De Jesus, 2006, pp. 412–413). There is a conscious link of academic content with the cultural and ethnic lives of students, especially the use of relevant materials (Antrop-Gonzalez, 2006; Blair, 2002; Galletta & Ayala, 2008; Scanlan & Lopez, 2012). Underlying this perspective is an embedded belief that "students bring something of value to contribute to the curriculum" (Ancess, 2003, p. 99) as well as "a commitment to provide students with important historical knowledge grounded in their identities" (Antrop-Gonzalez & De Jesus, 2006, p. 417). Schools marked by cultural relevance assume an additive approach to schooling (Antrop-Gonzalez, 2006; Steele 1997).

While there is little research to date collected on the outcomes of culturally relevant curriculum, there is strong theoretical evidence that students are advantaged when cultural relevance becomes a reality in schools (Jordan & Cooper, 2003; Leithwood, Jantzi, & Steinbach, 1999). On the question of intermediate outcomes, logic holds that relevant curricular standards and materials will enhance student integration into the school, social capital, self-esteem, and motivation (Antrop-Gonzalez, 2006; Scanlan & Lopez, 2012). These enhancements lead to heightened student engagement (Ancess, 2003), which in turn is associated theoretically and empirically with strengthened academic skills and better achievement scores (Murphy & Torre, 2014).

Program Coherence

The third domain of curriculum to which leaders need to attend is *coherence* and alignment (Wellisch, MacQueen, Carriere, & Duck, 1978) or what Murphy, Weil, Hallinger, and Mitman (1985) have called "tightly coupled curriculum" (p. 367). We preface this work with some important reminders: To begin with, we see that curriculum coherence is nested in the larger concept of overall "organizational integration" (Youngs & King, 2002, p. 646). This operational coherence addresses the extent to which the various systems and domains of the school are integrated and are all pulling in the same direction (Balfanz, Herzog, & MacIver, 2007; Stringfield & Reynolds, 2012). One way to describe this has been provided by Mitchell and Sackney (2006), who talk about "the degree of order within and consistency across various directions and instructional movements in a school" (p. 422). On this point, Robinson (2007) notes the "importance of overall guidance through a common set of principles and key ideas" (p. 13). Another strategy is to focus on the cohesion among systems and areas of work such as personnel management, instructional program, school operations, support activities, student services, and so forth. Here, we see a school that "operates more as an organizing whole and less as a loose collection of disparate systems" (Murphy, 1992, p. 98). Bryk and team (2010) put the direction and systems strategies together in the concept of "strategic orientation" (p. 63). *Strategic orientation* creates a theory of action for how and why actions work and provides a center of gravity for the various systems so they all hold together (Murphy, 1992; Murphy et al., 1985). In so doing, each of the domains and systems takes on life beyond itself. Each ends up touching one or more of the other domains (Spillane, Diamond, Walker, Halverson, & Jita, 2001).

As we move to understand the concept of organizational integration, we see a theme woven throughout this volume. That is, principals play the central role in bringing alignment, coherence, and integration to life in schools (Murphy, 1990a; Robinson, Lloyd, & Rowe, 2008). Where cohesion is found, the fingerprints of principals are universally visible (Marzano, Waters, & McNulty, 2005). The principal is the critical gluing agent, the person who gets things to cohere or permits them to operate in isolated fashion (Anderson, Moore, & Sun, 2009; Newmann, Smith, Allensworth, & Bryk, 2001). We would also be wise to remember that organizational coherence is not the norm in schools. Problems of continuity are inherent (Newmann, King, & Youngs, 2000). Most people work hard to run their own piece of the overall operation (e.g., a fifth-grade classroom, a library). "Everyone [is] kind of in their own world doing their own thing" (Eilers & Camacho, 2007, p. 624). The weaving of threads of connection is generally only a small part of that work. In addition, new ideas, programs, and reforms are often grafted onto rather than integrated into schools (Murphy, 2013a, 2013b). Adoption proceeds absent coordination (Newmann et al., 2001). Even on the occasions when they do migrate into the school, linkages to existing operations, programs, and people are often an afterthought: overload, fragmentation, and isolation are often dominant conditions.

We turn the lens now directly onto the topic of curriculum coherence. There are a number of ways to link content together and various methods for leaders to engage program integration and alignment. An important strategy has to do with creating alignment between the curriculum in special programs (e.g., special education, English language learners) and in the regular program. A second is the coordination of the curriculum with district and state standards and objectives (Johnson & Asera, 1999; Murphy, Hallinger, & Mesa, 1985). A third has to do with the classes where the curriculum unfolds: (a) in the integration of curriculum standards in a course, (b) in the same subject across classes (e.g., writing across the curriculum), (c) in the integration among classes in a discipline (i.e., sequenced program of study), (d) among subjects (e.g., science and history), and (e) within the alignment with higher-education courses (Bryk et al., 2010; Burch & Spillane, 2003; Kleiner & Lewis, 2005; Newmann et al., 2000). A fourth lens on curriculum coherence is to see through the experiences that occur for each student, whether they experience "academic drift and curricular debris" (Murphy, Hull, & Walker, 1987, p. 351) or well-cohered programs of study (Oakes & Guiton, 1995). Of special importance here is how well new material links to students' prior learning (Huberman, Parrish, Hannan, Arellanes, & Shambaugh, 2011). All of these aspects of curricular coherence find space in the idea of "curriculum mapping" (Eilers & Camacho, 2007, p. 614), "the subject matter that students are exposed to as they move across grades" (Bryk et al., 2010, p. 74).

There are also principles of operation and systems of support that influence curriculum alignment for better or worse. One is the linkage between school vision and goals and curricular content (Kruse, Seashore Louis, & Bryk, 1995; Spillane et al., 2001). As Leithwood and Montgomery (1982) reported at the start of the effective schools era, the difference between ineffective and effective school leaders on coordination of the curriculum was "the relatively precise focus of the effective principal on curriculum goals as the basis for integration rather than the more ambiguous diffuse goals of the typical principal on curriculum work being done in the school" (p. 324). Because "curriculum alignment is a social activity as well as a technical act" (Bryk et al., 2010, p. 117), the principle of collaborative teacher work in a reciprocal manner comes into play in the curriculum alignment narrative. Or, alternatively, curriculum alignment work is most productive in the context of professional learning communities. So we also see supportive policies around how time is allocated and protected in the curriculum coherence storyline (Eilers & Camacho, 2007; Firestone & Wilson, 1985). Relatedly, longer time commitments and consistent policy environments support program alignment (Desimone, 2002; Newmann et al., 2001). Finally, policies and guidelines that link resources and the curriculum help build alignment, especially in professional development (Halverson, Grigg, Prichett, & Thomas, 2007; Newmann et al., 2000).

ASSESSMENT

Assessment is the third point on the instructional program triangle, in combination with pedagogy and curriculum. While we address the technical dimension of assessment below, we are concerned primarily with exploring the overarching narrative of a climate or culture of inquiry (Eilers & Camacho, 2007; Halverson, et al., 2007), "a school environment conducive to data-based decision making" (Ingram, Seashore Louis, & Schroeder, 2004, p. 120). Supovitz and Klein (2003) refer to this conception of assessment as a "culture of systematic inquiry into the relationship between the instructional practices of teachers and the learning of their students" (p. 2). And Wohlstetter and colleagues (2008) remind us that this culture is about the development of widely shared norms and expectations about how data are employed.

Before we move into the main narrative here, we begin with our conclusions. To start, the research on effective schools and districts identifies well-crafted assessment as an explanatory variable in the success storyline (Kerr, Marsh, Ikemoto, Darilek, & Barney, 2006; Lachat & Smith, 2005). That is, we find that widespread and thoughtful use of data on student learning is essential in school improvement work and in enhancing the outcomes of that work, especially student academic achievement (Collins & Valentine, 2010).

Concomitantly, over the last 40 years, researchers have consistently found that principals are central figures in the growth of a culture of inquiry in schools. They are often the "driving force behind strong data use" (Supovitz & Klein, 2003, p. 36). They are key in setting goals for the use of assessment information (Levin & Datnow, 2012), helping establish a "press for using evidence" (Cosner, 2011, p. 291). They are assessment champions. Principals play a critical role in establishing an atmosphere of trust and collaboration that is a requirement of productive assessment systems. They provide support for teachers in collecting, analyzing, and using data and in turning numbers into action.

In the balance of our analysis of assessment, we take on five responsibilities. We begin with a discussion of the cultural and structural barriers that make meaningful assessment difficult to inculcate in many schools. In the second section, we examine the frames for building great assessment systems. We then turn to the essential elements and principles of productive assessment systems. In the fourth section, we analyze enabling supports. We conclude by unpacking the benefits of data-informed activities in schools.

Barriers

Cultural Discontinuities

The message that one derives from the research is that the current culture in schools is not conducive to data-driven assessment. That is, "the concept of data-based decision making . . . is unrealistic" (Ingram et al., 2004, p. 1283) in many schools and for large numbers of teachers. At a deep level, many educators do not view assessment as a "legitimate improvement strategy" (Young, 2006, p. 522). Ingram and team (2004) "surmise that being dismissive of externally generated achievement data is a cultural [marker] that teachers learn" (p. 1273). What this conveys is that the technical aspects of assessment are insufficient. In the average school, the use of data is formulaic, episodic, and superficial (Blanc et al., 2010; Ingram et al., 2004). As a result, "most teachers do not rely on data to examine the effectiveness of teaching. Changing this requires not only changes in behavior but also in deeply held values" (Ingram et al., 2004, p. 1281).

In schools today, we know that teachers have considerable mistrust of data and the use of data in schools. Consequently, they rarely embrace and often reject assessment information (Wayman & Stringfield, 2006). Teachers tend to see data quite differently than do analysts in the larger policy community. It is normal for them to question both the accuracy and validity of assessment systems as well as the resulting data (Kerr et al., 2006; Timperley, 2009). They often view assessment data as "inaccurate or not relevant to teacher concerns" (Lachat & Smith, 2005, p. 344). Teachers also see that, at times, data interfere with classroom work and is often in competition with instruction (Blase & Blase, 2004; Kerr et al., 2006). They often note that much of the data that assessment systems provide simply duplicates what they know already. Likewise, teachers often discern conflict between assessment and the curriculum. Assessments that count are sometimes viewed as forcing curricular compaction, necessitating the use of less robust curriculum (Datnow, Park, & Kennedy, 2008; Desimone,

2002). On other occasions, teachers find that the demands of curricular coverage make using data a moot point (Kerr et al., 2006).

Also ingrained in the teaching (and leadership) ranks is the belief that the real goal of much of the data machinery in place is not for the improvement of instruction but for compliance, accountability, or political ends, ends which teachers view as not benefitting classroom instruction (Blanc et al., 2010; Ingram et al., 2004; Young, 2006). Here, we often find not only a lack of trust but a sense of threat as well (Firestone & Martinez, 2007; Kerr et al., 2006). Teachers often see the data as a basis for others crafting professional judgments rather than as a foundation for constructive work—that is, as a vehicle to assign blame (Blanc et al., 2010; Halverson et al., 2007; Ingram et al., 2004).

Equally, if not more troubling, is the sense among some educators that "traditional assessments do not include or reflect what they perceive as valued and important outcomes . . . such as higher order thinking skills" (Desimone, 2002, p. 445). Thus, as Ingram and his colleagues (2004) have noted, "[T]eachers, even when they accept their state's testing and accountability system as necessary, don't view the test data as sufficient" (pp. 1281–1282). There is also, at times, a noticeable tension between modes of traditional assessment and professional judgment. Also discernible is an undercurrent that many of the topics and measures on which students desire information rest outside the realm of academic performance, regardless of how it is assessed (Cosner, 2011; Ingram et al., 2004). As we have reported elsewhere, there is a near vacuum of data on the half of schooling that deals with the critical dimension of care for students (Murphy & Torre, 2014). It is not unusual, therefore, for teachers to be "willing to bend to the narrower vision of academic outcomes alone" (Ingram et al., 2004, p. 1279).

Inadequate Support

There is considerable agreement that school people often lack the supports required to collect, analyze, and employ data either individually or in communities of practice. That is, they are not prepared to address the obstacles they confront (Ingram et al., 2004). Lack of time is the most troubling condition uncovered in the research. As noted above under cultural discontinuities, teachers often see assessment systems as stealing classroom time and interfering with their work with children. The absence of leadership is a common lament as well (Levin & Datnow, 2012); criticisms are molded in terms of formal school leaders who are not data literate as well as unskilled teacher leadership in professional communities. Lack of collective leadership is especially detrimental to sustainability (Wayman & Stringfield, 2006). Inadequate and unwieldy data systems are often seen, especially on the technology side (Datnow et al., 2008; Supovitz, 2002), promoting what Blanc and colleagues (2010) describe as a lack of "capacity for open discussion" (p. 216).

Compounding the obstacles of time and leadership is the reappearing conclusion that teachers and principals often lack the knowledge needed to handle well-crafted assessment systems (Kerr et al., 2006; Wayman & Stringfield, 2006). Or, as Brunner and team (n.d.) conclude, "[R]esearchers are hard pressed to find substantial numbers of educators who have adequate training and knowledge and are prepared to make appropriate use of data and transform it into useable information and practice" (p. 4). Ingram and associates (2004, p. 1280) conclude that while teachers are not data phobic and even when the culture is positive, "[T]hey don't have recent experience in working with data to improve specific classroom practices." Limited preparation, inadequate mentoring by principals, and lack of capacity at the district level are each underscored in this storyline (Blanc et al., 2010; Lachat & Smith 2005).

Data systems routinely present obstacles for schools. Teachers believe that they are often inundated with data, receive data in unsophisticated forms, and lack strategies to process information (Ingram et al., 2004; Kerr et al., 2006). There are many places, teachers remind us, where timelines in receiving assessment data are less than desirable (Datnow et al., 2008). A consistent complaint is that data are not adequately aligned to the curriculum unfolding in classrooms, a return to our earlier point about teachers questioning the meaningfulness of external assessments.

Frames for Assessment

In this section, we begin our discussion of planning or agenda-setting assessment with some notes about the deep essentials of the work and describe the reciprocal cycle of assessment (Young, 2006). We then delve deeply into the steps of that recursive, overlapping cycle. Our first observation is that all stages of the system need to unfold for assessment to work well (Blanc et al., 2010; Datnow et al., 2008). Great collection and weak analysis will not work well. Neither will excellent analysis and poor use of data. Secondly, planning for data-based activity is essential; it makes the assessment process efficient and effective (Kerr et al., 2006). Third, as Young (2006) reveals, working on the technical and rational aspects of assessment alone is insufficient to garner important gains. Without simultaneous attention to values and norms around assessment, meaning and relevance are too easily left out of the equation, a recipe for producing formulaic work (Blanc et al., 2010; Collins & Valentine, 2010). Fourth, it is generally helpful to begin with the end in mind and then work backwards (Supovitz, 2002). Lastly, the issues of guiding principles and supports will have considerable influence in determining how effective we are in crafting productive assessment systems.

We move now to the discussion of the four stages in the cyclical process or "cybernetic cycle" (Scheerens, 1997, p. 276) of assessment: determining the goals or purposes of assessment and identifying the data of importance; collecting and managing data; analyzing and sensemaking; and using data.

While the information from assessment "can be a powerful ally in stimulating positive change and improvement" (Lachat & Smith, 2005, p. 333) and without data, there is blindness in school improvement work (Blase & Blase, 2000; Datnow et al., 2008), the starting position for us is that "unless . . . agreement can be reached among stakeholders on fundamental goals, there will be little agreement on what constitutes meaningful data" (Ingram et al., 2004, p. 1273). Goals precede collection and analysis and are, in turn, informed by assessment data (Brunner et al., n.d.; Wohlstetter et al., 2008). Absent this perspective, data can "inadvertently compromise the overarching purpose of data-driven practice" (Datnow et al., 2008, p. 8).

At the macro level, data can be placed in the service of learning and/or holding students and education responsible for outcomes (Riester, Pursch, & Skria, 2002). On the learning front, analysts have shown us that data can be employed for an assortment of purposes, almost all of which are linked to strengthening the instructional program (Blanc et al., 2010; Supovitz, 2002). Researchers illuminate three overlapping sets of learning purposes:

> Student achievement data can be used for various purposes, including evaluating progress toward state and district standards, monitoring student performance and improvement, determining where assessments converge and diverge, and judging the efficacy of local curriculum and instructional practices. (Wohlstetter et al., 2008, p. 240)

> We have identified seven major ways in which teachers and administrators in our sample explained how they used student performance data for instructional or organizational improvement. First and foremost, they used student performance data to inform instruction. . . . Second, they used data specifically to identify low-performing students and inform assistance plans for these students. . . . Third, they used data to plan professional development. . . . Fourth, they used data to set targets and goals. . . . Fifth, they used data to celebrate both faculty and student accomplishments. . . . Sixth, they used data as a visual means of reinforcing school priorities and focus. . . . Seventh, data were used as supporting evidence in conversations with parents about students. (Supovitz, 2002, pp. 13–15)

> Studies have documented a multitude of purposes toward which schools have successfully applied data-based inquiry. Most commonly, data are used for tasks such as setting annual and intermediate goals as part of the school improvement process. Data may also be used to visually depict goals and visions, motivate students and staff, and celebrate achievement and improvement. Schools use data for instructional decisions such as identifying standards, refining course offerings, identifying low-performing students, and monitoring student progress. School structure, policy, and resource

use may be informed by data. Schools have also used data for decisions related to personnel, such as evaluating team performance and determining and refining topics for professional development. (Kerr et al., 2006, p. 498)

Embedded in these three summaries is affirmation of the central theme that goals drive data collection and that data collection, in turn, shapes goals. We also see confirmation of the two core assessment pathways to build schools as academic place: strengthening the quality of the instructional program and enhancing student academic performance (Kerr et al., 2006; Riester et al., 2002). In each of these pathways, particular emphasis is placed on identifying and addressing student weaknesses in relation to standards (Cosner, 2011; Gray et al., 1999; Rumberger, 2011). Researchers report that this ongoing and meaningful use of performance information fosters (1) a "culture of inquiry" in schools (Datnow et al., 2008, p. 10)—a culture defined by teacher ownership of data—and (2) collaborative decisions on the allocation of resources (Blanc et al., 2010; Brunner et al., n.d.; Levin & Datnow, 2012).

According to analysts who study assessment, the second leg in the inquiry process is data collection or data acquisition, to which we would add managing the data (Halverson et al., 2007; Lachat & Smith, 2005; McDougall, Saunders, & Goldenberg, 2007). Key ingredients here include collection in the service of purpose and goals; the use of multiple sources of information; and ongoing, regular collection activities (Cotton, 2003; Supovitz & Klein, 2003). Digital technology is especially helpful at this stage both with the collection and managing data work (Brunner et al., n.d.). Collecting, managing, and storing data carries us to the questions of which data will be collected and how (e.g., survey, tests, observations) (Cotton, 2003). Research here reminds us that data need to be well organized and easily accessible if gathering efforts are to bear fruit. The important issue of displaying data merits noting here as well (Blanc et al., 2010).

Keeping in mind that there is considerable overlap among the steps or stages of the cyclical assessment process, we turn now to data analysis. Our work convinces us that the essential issue here is *sensemaking*, the process employed to develop an understanding of what data tell us (Blanc et al., 2010; Halverson et al., 2007). A key point to hold in mind here is that data often do not provide answers. They point in certain directions, raise questions, and help open possibilities (Allensworth & Easton, 2005; Kerr et al., 2006). The interpretation of the data holds high ground and that work is predicated on what educators know. Data can also be complex and messy, leading to the emergence of alternative explanations and avenues of action (Supovitz & Klein, 2003). The defining process in the transformation is interrogation (e.g., disaggregation, reflection, and discourse), paying special attention to the different messages that the data convey (Murphy, 2010; Supovitz & Klein, 2003; Young, 2006).

Making sense of data is the prelude to the next phase of the assessment cycle, constructive use of data or "taking action based on what [was] learned" (Supovitz & Klein, 2003, p. 33). This includes the "willingness to change instructional practice in the face of new information" (Halverson et al., 2007, p. 17). Data use exposes the recursive nature of the assessment cycle. It depends on the previous phase, *data analysis*; that is to say, "the type of data collected determine the type of decisions that are made" (Lachat & Smith, 2005, p. 335). It is employed in the service of the first phase of the cycle (goals and purposes). It leads directly back to phase two of the cycle as well (i.e., the collection of data at this point concerning the success of actions taken to improve the school). And the cycle is set in consistent motion.

Elements and Principles

Research underscores the essential elements and principles of productive systems. While these ingredients are blended in schools and districts, we pull them apart for analysis. We discuss them under the following descriptors: actionable, coherent, and professionally anchored.

Actionable assessment systems, as noted above, are purpose driven and goal driven. *Actionable* also means that assessment programs are understandable (i.e., user friendly) and that the information produced is valid, relevant, and useful (Datnow et al., 2008; Kerr et al., 2006). Actionable systems offer guidance and concrete data (Hayes, Christie, Mills, & Lingard, 2004; Wayman & Stringfield, 2006). There is efficiency in access to data. Teachers view the data as necessary (Levin & Datnow, 2012). It allows them to see "how they [can] address emerging issues in their classrooms" (Halverson et al., 2007, p. 41). It pushes the spotlight onto instruction. In the words of Wayman and Stringfield (2006), actionable systems "help teachers use data rather than being used by data" (p. 569). Data are accessible but not intrusive (Friedkin & Slater, 1994). Information is made available in a timely manner (Kerr et al., 2006; Lachat & Smith, 2005) to "enable teachers to quickly analyze data for instructional decision making" (Datnow et al., 2008, p. 32). Actionable systems provide comparable data (Blanc et al., 2010). There is a focus on authentic measures of demonstrating learning (Bryk et al., 2010). They promote the unpacking and disaggregation of data (Lachat & Smith, 2005; Murphy, 2010).

Analysts routinely describe a second element of productive assessment systems—coherence—as well as the principles that help define the element. Cohesiveness covers a good deal of space in the assessment narrative and overlaps with the other two essential elements, actionability and professional integration. One principle of integration is the continuous nature of assessments (Huberman et al., 2011; Kerr et al., 2006). Another is the reliance on a comprehensive platform of both internal and external forms of data collection and the systems collection of data (Ingram et al.,

2004). Coherent assessment features multiple and varied types of data to provide insights into quality instruction and student learning (Lachat & Smith, 2005; Leithwood, 2008).

A core principle here is that there is "breadth and depth to data-related functions" (Young, 2006, p. 544). That is, coherence arises in part from multiple and overlapping functions. Mayrowetz and Weinstein (1999, p. 423) capture this aspect of coherence when they report that redundancy is a critical dimension of productive assessment systems. Another principle highlights the linkage between assessment and the larger task of school improvement (Hallinger & Murphy, 1985). Because data-driven decision making is not something that can be brought to life in isolation, in cohesive assessment systems, these two domains are intricately linked (Datnow et al., 2008; Lachat & Smith, 2005). We also find in a coherent world that adult learning and assessment are deeply intertwined (Murphy, Elliot, Goldring, & Porter, 2007; Murphy, Hallinger, Weil, & Mitman, 1983). Coherence here also means that there is planned alignment between assessments and the other domains of the instructional program, such as curriculum and instruction (Hallinger & Murphy, 1986; Wohlstetter et al., 2008).

This final element carries us into the domain of *culture*, what we refer to as a professionally anchored assessment system (Datnow et al., 2008; Young, 2006). Cosner (2011, p. 794) characterizes this as "an inquiry-oriented schoolwide culture," a climate in which "using data to guide instruction become[s] a habit of mind for teachers" (Cooper, Ponder, Merritt, & Matthews, 2005, p. 12). There is a culture of collective development of and use of assessment systems and the resulting data (Wohlstetter et al., 2008; Young, 2006). Here, we find teachers that talk more "of collaboration that [is] academic and professional" (Wayman & Stringfield, 2006, p. 565). In professionally anchored assessment systems, "teachers are provided with opportunities to work collaboratively in building their capacity to use data" (Lachat & Smith, 2005, p. 236). "Norms of interaction" (Young, 2006, p. 540) and deprivatization hold high ground where professional grounded assessment cultures flourish (Louis, Marks, & Kruse, 1996; Murphy & Torre, 2014). Collaborative work and learning norms are underscored (Halverson et al., 2007; Murphy, 2015). The reflective sensemaking we explored earlier is a sense of ownership of results from data collection and analysis, teachers coming together to see that the data are their data (Lachat & Smith, 2005; Levin & Datnow, 2012). The front side of this ownership is commitment and sense of responsibility for student learning (Johnson & Asera, 1999; Murphy, 2015), a collective and "overwhelming consensus about the importance of using data to improve teacher performance and student achievement" (Datnow et al., 2008, p. 5). The back end is mutual accountability (Murphy & Torre, 2014; Wohlstetter et al., 2008), "a community that holds its members accountable for learning" (Young, 2006, p. 538).

Enabling Supports

Supports are the next piece in the assessment system. Support includes leadership, resources, and systems and structures—"school conditions and practices that . . . promote staff use of data" (Lachat & Smith, 2005, p. 334). We begin with the central theme of the book: Leadership is a required support for productive assessment systems to take root and grow (Beck & Murphy, 1996; Hallinger & Murphy, 2013). In the best sense of the term, leaders are "instigators" (Supovitz & Klein, 2003, p. 2) and advocates and champions (Lachat & Smith, 2005). In a real sense, leadership helps the other supports to materialize (Murphy et al., 2001). The research illuminates a number of important leadership activities, all of which center on creating organizational capacity:

> Leadership focused on data use or agenda setting affects teachers' impetus for using data and correspondingly loosens or tightens the connections between data-driven rhetoric and teachers' data practices. (Young, 2006, p. 532)

> Principals have been found to be pivotal in modeling effective data use and in enabling teachers to use technology. Principals are also critical in providing ongoing learning opportunities for teachers to discuss and analyze their students' data. (Levin & Datnow, 2012, p. 180)

> Four roles individually enacted by principals include (a) establishing, communicating, and reinforcing an evidence-based agenda and necessary work tasks, (b) modeling data use and maintaining an organizational routine that [make] public the practice of evidence-based grade-level collaboration, (c) buffering and filtering the school from the district in ways that support evidence-based grade-level collaboration, and (d) supporting and shaping shared leadership in service of evidence-based grade-level collaboration. (Cosner, 2011, p. 801)

Leaders in schools and districts with effective assessment systems are key in getting the goals of measurement in place (Blanc et al., 2010; Supovitz & Klein, 2003). They are often in a unique position to move financial and human resources to assessment work, especially individual and collective capacity-building activities (Blanc et al., 2010; Lachat & Smith, 2005; Wayman & Stringfield, 2006).

In robust assessment programs, we see considerable energy linked to the following interconnected resources: money, time, people, training, and tools. Where assessment works well, money is dedicated to developing the required pieces of the continuous data system (Brunner et al., n.d.; Cosner, 2011). Funds are set aside to provide time for teachers to learn about the workings of assessment programs (Young, 2006). Ample time for collaborative work is routinely cited in the research (Ingram et al., 2004). Time to collect, analyze, and put data to use is essential (Kerr et al., 2006; Wayman & Stringfield, 2006). Particularly salient is "furnishing instructional resources linked to issues arising from data analysis" (Young, 2006, p. 540) and helping teachers to master more effective teaching strategies (Dannetta, 2002; Datnow et al., 2008). At a more concrete level, resources include tools and protocols to use with the data system and in turning information into more effective instruction (Kerr et al., 2006; Levin & Datnow, 2012).

Also important is time for professional development, the building of individual and collective knowledge and skills in the assessment domain (Blase & Kirby, 2009; Cosner, 2011) or the "building of strong human capacity for data-driven inquiry" (Kerr et al., 2006, p. 498). Targeted assistance or "data support personnel" (Datnow et al., 2008, p. 34) is a resource in the area of professional development often seen in the assessment research. Here, we find the provision of help in the form of data coaches and opportunities to work on data teams (Kerr et al., 2006). This work is designed to mentor "teachers in managing and using data" (Datnow et al., 2008, p. 34). This type of mentoring is sometimes extended to include the new instructional practices that derive from thoughtful use of data (Johnson & Asera, 1999; Young, 2006). Overall then, we find time being devoted to understanding the data system and to learning how to strengthen teaching and learning (Kerr et al., 2006; Young, 2006).

The final resource is the presence of a well-developed system of assessment that guides data-based inquiry (Kerr et al., 2006), what Cosner (2011) calls "enabling organizational conditions that offer support for the substantive inquiry-oriented work embedded in evidence-based collaboration" (p. 793). Halverson and colleagues (2007, p. 4) refer to this support as a "data-driven instructional system" while Kerr and team (2006, p. 508) call it a "data management system." We know that these systems attend to both the "infrastructure and methods" of assessment (Datnow et al., 2008, p. 32), especially the needed structural supports (Lachat & Smith, 2005; Levin & Datnow, 2012). These structures provide frameworks for the data collection inquiry cycle (McDougall et al., 2007; Supovitz & Klein, 2003), frameworks that are essential to "establish[ing] coherent and high-level data-system capability" (Lachat & Smith, 2005, p. 336).

Benefits

Assessment systems that work to address the barriers outlined earlier and that adhere to the elements and principles noted immediately above are expected to have positive impacts on teacher and students. The theory of action and the empirical evidence that powers this assumption rely on the creation of more effective schools by strengthening teaching and learning. The end point in this theoretical and conceptual chain is that "when teachers use in-depth analysis of assessment information to assist them to modify their [program], student achievement is raised" (Robinson, 2007, p. 15). That is, "previous research suggests that data-driven decision making has the potential to increase student performance" (Wohlstetter et al., 2008, p. 239).

The intermediate point between productive assessment and student learning is more informed, more responsive, and more effective teaching. More specifically, research on teacher perceptions reveals that well-grounded assessment systems lead to a number of improved conditions. There is an increased sense of clarity about teaching, a stronger sense of focus in general and an enhanced focus on student learning and success in particular (Lachat & Smith, 2005; Stringfield & Reynolds, 2012). Professionalism grows (Wayman & Stringfield, 2006) and, as Datnow (2008) explains, "[S]tudies indicate that effective use of data . . . enhances the ability of schools to become learning organizations" (p. 10). In important ways, there is a tightening up of the looseness of instructional practice in schools (Bryk et al., 2010). Data focus attention, concentration, and action (Blanc et al., 2010). Especially important here is that teachers often get to know their students better (Supovitz & Klein, 2003). A productive assessment system "allow[s] them a deeper and more rounded view of their students' learning" (Wayman & Stringfield, 2006, p. 563) and more "detailed pictures of their students' strengths and weaknesses" (Johnson & Asera, 1999, pp. 146–147). This leads to "improved identification of students' learning needs" (Kerr et al., 2006, p. 501), particularly the requirements of students "who are in need of additional assistance" (Supovitz & Klein, 2003, p. 19). The use of data to identify needs is associated with more and better responses to those needs (Wayman & Stringfield, 2006). This includes increases in expectations and more appropriate diversification and differentiation of instruction, including more productive use of student groups (Datnow et al., 2008; Gray et al., 1999; Johnson & Asera, 1999; Wayman & Stringfield, 2006). Concomitantly, highly functional data systems allow teachers to discern their effectiveness with greater clarity and validity (Supovitz & Klein, 2003).

References

Adams, C. (2010). Social determinants of student trust in high poverty elementary schools. In W. K. Hoy & M. DiPaola (Eds.), *Analyzing school contexts: Influences of principals and teachers in the service of students* (pp. 255–280). Charlotte, NC: Information Age.

Ainscow, M., & Southworth, G. (1996). School improvement: A study of the roles of leaders and external consultants. *School Effectiveness and School Improvement, 7*(3), 229–251.

Alder, N. (2002). Interpretations of the meaning of care: Creating caring relationships in urban middle school classrooms. *Urban Education, 37*(2), 241–266.

Alexander, K. L., & Cook, M. A. (1982). Curricula and coursework: A surprise ending to a familiar story. *American Sociological Review, 47*(5), 626–640.

Alexander, K. L., Cook, M., & McDill, E. L. (1978). Curriculum tracking and educational stratification: Some further evidence. *American Sociological Review, 43*, 47–66.

Alexander, K. L., & McDill, E. L. (1976). Selection and allocation within schools: Some causes and consequences of curriculum placement. *American Sociological Review, 41*, 936–980.

Allensworth, E. M., & Easton, J. Q. (2005). *The on-track indicator as a predictor of high school graduation.* Chicago, IL: Consortium on Chicago School Research at the University of Chicago.

Ancess, J. (2000). The reciprocal influence of teacher learning, teaching practice, school restructuring, and student learning outcomes. *The Teachers College Record, 102*(3), 590–619.

Ancess, J. (2003). *Beating the odds: High schools as communities of commitment.* New York, NY: Teachers College Press.

Anderson, R. C., Hiebert, E. H., Scott, J. A., & Wilkinson, I. A. G. (1985). *Becoming a nation of readers: The report of the Commission on Reading.* Washington, DC: The National Institute of Education, U.S. Department of Education.

Anderson, S., Moore, S., & Sun, J. (2009). Positioning the principals in patterns of school leadership distribution. In K. Leithwood, B. Mascall, & T. Strauss (Eds.), *Distributed leadership according to the evidence* (pp. 111–136). London, England: Routledge.

Antrop-Gonzalez, R. (2006). Toward the school as sanctuary concept in multicultural urban education: Implications for small high school reform. *Curriculum Inquiry, 36*(3), 273–301.

Antrop-Gonzalez, R., & De Jesus, A. (2006). Toward a theory of critical care in urban small school reform: Examining structures and pedagogies of caring in two Latino community-based schools. *International Journal of Qualitative Studies in Education, 19*(4), 409–433.

Askew, B. J., Fountas, I. C., Lyons, C. A., Pinnell, G. S., & Schmitt, M. C. (2000). A review of Reading Recovery. In R. D. Robinson, M. C. McKenna, & J. M. Wedman (Eds.), *Issues and trends in literacy education* (2nd ed., pp. 284–303). Needham Heights, MA: Allyn & Bacon.

Askew, B. J., & Gaffney, J. S. (1999). Reading recovery: Waves of influence on literacy education. In J. S. Gaffney & B. J. Askew (Eds.), *Stirring the waters: The influence of Marie Clay* (pp. 75–98). Portsmouth, NH: Heinemann.

Au, K. H., & Asam, C. L. (1996). Improving the literacy achievement of low-income students of diverse backgrounds. In M. F. Graves, P. van der Broek, & B. M. Taylor (Eds.), *The first R: Every child's right to read* (pp. 199–223). New York, NY: Teachers College Press.

Auerbach, S. (2007). Visioning parent engagement in urban schools. *Journal of School Leadership, 17*(6), 699–734.

Auerbach, S. (2009). Walking the walk: Portraits in leadership for family engagement in urban schools. *School Community Journal, 19*(1), 9–32.

Baker, J. A., Terry, T., Briger, R., & Winsor, A. (1997). School as caring communities: A relational approach to school reform. *The School Psychology Review, 26*(4), 586–602.

Balfanz, R., Herzog, L., & MacIver, D. (2007). Preventing student disengagement and keeping students on the graduation path in urban middle-grades schools: Early identification and effective interventions. *Educational Psychologist, 42*(4), 223–235.

Barnes, C. A., Camburn, E., Sanders, B. R., & Sebastian, J. (2010). Developing instructional leaders: Using mixed methods to explore the black box of planned change in principals' professional practice. *Educational Administration Quarterly, 46*(2), 241–279.

Barnett, K., & McCormick, J. (2004). Leadership and individual principal-teacher relationships in schools. *Educational Administration Quarterly, 40*(3), 406–434.

Barnett, K., McCormick, J., & Conners, R. (2001). Transformational leadership in schools: Panacea, placebo, or problem? *Journal of Educational Administration, 39*(1), 24–46.

Barton, P. E. (2003). Parsing the achievement gap. *Policy Information Report*. Princeton, NJ: Educational Testing Service.

Beachum, F., & Dentith, A. M. (2004). Teacher leaders creating cultures of school renewal and transformation. *Educational Forum, 68*(3), 276–286.

Beck, L. G., & Foster, W. (1999). Administration and community: Considering challenges, exploring possibilities. In J. Murphy & K. S. Louis (Eds.), *Handbook of research on educational administration* (pp. 337–358). San Francisco, CA: Jossey-Bass.

Beck, L. G., & Murphy, J. (1992). *Understanding the principalship: A metaphorical analysis, 1960–1990*. San Francisco, CA: Jossey-Bass.

Beck, L. G., & Murphy, J. (1996). *The four imperatives of a successful school*. Newbury Park, CA: Corwin.

Becker, B. E., & Luthar, S. S. (2002). Social-emotional factors affecting achievement outcomes among disadvantaged students: Closing the achievement gap. *Educational Psychologist, 37*(4), 197–214.

Beers, D., & Ellig, J. (1994). An economic view of the effectiveness of public and private schools. In S. Hakim, P. Seidenstat, & G. W. Bowman (Eds.), *Privatizing education and educational choice: Concepts, plans, and experiences* (pp. 19–38). Westport, CT: Praeger.

Berends, M., Lucas, S. R., Sullivan, T., & Briggs, R. J. (2005). *Examining gaps in mathematics achievement among racial-ethnic groups, 1972–1992.* Santa Monica, CA: Rand Corporation.

Betts, J., Zau, A., & Koedel, C. (2010). *Lessons in reading reform: Finding what works.* San Francisco, CA: Public Policy Institute of California.

Bishop, H. L., Tinley, A., & Berman, B. T. (1997). A contemporary leadership model to promote teacher leadership. *Action in Teacher Education, 19*(3), 77–81.

Blair, M. (2002). Effective school leadership: The multi-ethnic context. *British Journal of Sociology of Education,* 179–191.

Blanc, S., Christman, J. B., Liu, R., Mitchell, C., Travers, E., & Bulkley, K. E. (2010). Learning to learn from data: Benchmarks and instructional communities. *Peabody Journal of Education, 85*(2), 205–225.

Blase, J., & Blase, J. (1999). Principals' instructional leadership and teacher development: Teachers' perspectives. *Educational Administration Quarterly, 35*(3), 349–378.

Blase, J., & Blase, J. (2000). Effective instructional leadership: Teachers' perspectives on how principals promote teaching and learning in schools. *Journal of Educational Administration, 38*(2), 130–141.

Blase, J., & Blase, J. (2004). *Handbook of instructional leadership: How really good principals promote teaching and learning.* Thousand Oaks, CA: Corwin.

Blase, J., & Kirby, P. (2009). *Bringing out the best in teachers: What effective principals do.* Thousand Oaks, CA: Corwin.

Blegen, M. B., & Kennedy, C. (2000). Principals and teachers, leading together. *NASSP Bulletin, 84*(616), 1–6.

Blumenfeld, P., Fishman, B. J., Krajcik, J., Marx, R. W., & Soloway, E. (2000). Creating usable innovations in systemic reform: Scaling up technology embedded project based science in urban schools. *Educational Psychologist, 35*(3), 149–164.

Boles, K., & Troen, V. (1996). Teacher leaders and power: Achieving school reform from the classroom. In G. Moller & M. Katzenmeyer (Eds.), *Every teacher as a leader: Realizing the potential of teacher leadership* (pp. 41–62). San Francisco, CA: Jossey-Bass.

Bolman, L., & Deal, T. (2008). *Reframing organizations: Artistry, choice and leadership.* San Francisco, CA: Jossey-Bass.

Borko, H. (2004). Professional development and teacher learning: Mapping the terrain. *Educational Researcher, 33*(8), 3–15.

Borman, G. D., & Kimball, S. M. (2005). Teacher quality and educational equality: Do teachers with higher standards-based evaluation ratings close student achievement gaps? *The Elementary School Journal, 106*(1), 3–20.

Branch, G., Hanushek, E., & Rivkin, S. (2012). *Estimating the effect of leaders on public sector productivity: The case of school principals.* Working Paper 66. Washington, DC: National Center for Analysis of Longitudinal Data in Education Research.

Branch, G., Rivkin, S., & Hanushek, E. (2003). School leaders matter: Measuring the impact of effective principals. *Education Next, 13*(1), 1–8.

Brewer, D. J. (1993). Principals and student outcomes: Evidence from US high schools. *Economics of Education Review*, *12*(4), 281–292.

Brookover, W. B., Beady, C., Flood, P., Schweitzer, J., & Wisenbaker, J. (1979). *School social systems and student achievement: Schools can make a difference*. New York, NY: Praeger.

Brookover, W. B., & Lezotte, L. W. (1977). *Changes in school characteristics coincident with changes in student achievement*. East Lansing: College of Urban Development, Michigan State University.

Brookover, W. B., Schweitzer, J. J., Schneider, J. M., Beady, C. H., Flood, P. K., & Wisenbaker, J. M. (1978). Elementary school social climate and school achievement. *American Educational Research Journal*, *15*(2), 301–318.

Brooks, J. S., Scribner, J. P., & Eferakorho, J. (2004). Teacher leadership in the context of whole school reform. *Journal of School Leadership*, *14*(3), 242–265.

Brown, J., & Sheppard, B. (1999). *Leadership, organizational learning, and classroom change*. Paper presented at the annual meeting of the American Educational Research Association, Montreal, Quebec, Canada.

Brunner, C., Fasca, C., Heinze, J., Honey, M., Light, D., Mandinach, E., & Wexler, D. (n.d.). *Linking data and learning: The grow network study*. New York, NY: Education Development Center.

Bryk, A. S., Sebring, P. B., Allensworth, E., Luppescu, S., & Easton, J. (2010). *Organizing schools for improvement: Lessons from Chicago*. Chicago, IL: University of Chicago Press.

Bulkley, K. E., & Hicks, J. (2005). Managing community: Professional community in charter schools operated by educational management organizations. *Educational Administration Quarterly*, *41*(2), 306–348.

Burch, P., & Spillane, J. P. (2003). Elementary school leadership strategies and subject matter: Reforming mathematics and literacy instruction. *The Elementary School Journal*, 519–535.

Burke, C. (1992). Devolution of responsibility to Queensland schools: Clarifying the rhetoric critiquing the reality. *Journal of Educational Administration*, *30*(4), 33–52.

Burns, J. M. (1978). *Leadership*. New York, NY: Harper & Row.

Burns, R., Keyes, M., & Kusimo, P. (2005). *Closing achievement gaps by creating culturally responsive schools*. Charleston, WV: Appalachia Educational Lab.

Caldwell, B. J. (1998). Strategic leadership, resource management and effective school reform. *Journal of Educational Administration*, *36*(5), 445–461.

Camara, W. J., & Schmidt, A. E. (1999). *Group differences in standardized testing and social stratification*. (College Board Report No. 99–5). New York, NY: The College Board.

Carbonaro, W., & Gamoran, A. (2002). The production of achievement inequality in high school English. *American Educational Research Journal*, *39*(4), 801–827.

Center for Teaching Quality. (2007). *Teaching and learning conditions improve high school reform efforts*. Chapel Hill, NC: Author.

Chavis, G., Ward, L., Elwell, T., & Barret, C. (1997). *Improving student performance in high poverty schools*. Report Number: 96-86. Tallahassee, FL: Office of Program Policy Analysis and Government Accountability.

Childs-Bowen, D., Moller, C., & Scrivner, J. (2000, May). Principals: Leaders of leaders. *NASSP Bulletin*, *84*(6), 27–34.

Christle, C. A., Jolivette, K., & Nelson, C. M. (2005). Breaking the school to prison pipeline: Identifying school risk and protective factors for youth delinquency. *Exceptionality*, *13*(2), 69–88.

Clark, C., Dyson, A., Millward, A., & Robson, S. (1999). Theories of inclusion, theories of schools: Deconstructing and reconstructing the "inclusive school." *British Educational Research Journal, 25*(2), 157–177.

Cochran-Smith, M., & Lytle, S. (1999). Relationship of knowledge and practice: Teacher learning in communities. In A. Iran-Nejad & C. D. Pearson (Eds.), *Review of research in education.* (Vol. 24, pp. 249–306). Washington, DC: American Educational Research Association.

Coldren, A. F., & Spillane, J. P. (2007). Making connections to teaching practice: The role of boundary practices in instructional leadership. *Educational Policy, 2*(21), 369–396.

Collins, J., & Valentine, J. (2010). *Testing the impact of student engagement on standardized achievement: An empirical study of the influence of classroom engagement on test scores across school types.* Paper presented at the Annual Meeting of the University Council for Education Administration, New Orleans, LA.

Conchas, G. (2001). Structuring failure and success: Understanding the variability in Latino school engagement. *Harvard Educational Review, 71*(3), 475–505.

Cook-Sather, A. (2006). Sound, presence, and power: "Student voice" in educational research and reform. *Curriculum Inquiry, 36*(4), 359–390.

Cooley, V. E., & Shen, J. (2003). School accountability and professional job responsibilities: A perspective from secondary principals. *NASSP Bulletin, 87*(634), 10–25.

Cooper, J., Ponder, G., Merritt, S., & Matthews, C. (2005). High-performing high schools: Patterns of success. *NASSP Bulletin, 89*(645), 2–23.

Cooper, R. (1996). Detracking reform in an urban California high school: Improving the schooling experiences of African American students. *Journal of Negro Education, 2*(65), 190–208.

Cooper, R. (2000, January). Urban school reform from a student-of-color perspective. *Urban Education, 34*(5), 597–622.

Cosner, S. (2009). Building organizational capacity through trust. *Educational Administration Quarterly, 45*(2), 248–291.

Cosner, S. (2011). Supporting the initiation and early development of evidence-based grade-level collaboration in urban elementary schools: Key roles and strategies of principals and literacy coordinators. *Urban Education, 46*(4), 786–827.

Cotton, K. (2000). *The schooling practices that matter most.* Alexandria, VA: Association for Supervision and Curriculum Development.

Cotton, K. (2003). *Principals and student achievement: What the research says.* Alexandria, VA: Association for Supervision and Curriculum Development.

Craig, C. (2009). Research in the midst of organized school reform: Versions of teacher community in tension. *American Educational Research Journal, 46*(2), 598–619.

Creemers, B. P. M., & Reezigt, G. J. (1996). School level conditions affecting the effectiveness of instruction. *School Effectiveness and School Improvement, 7*(3), 197–228.

Cremin, L. A. (1955). The revolution in American secondary education, 1893–1918. *Teachers College Record, 56*(6), 295–308.

Cremin, L. A. (1961). *The transformation of the school: Progressivism in American education 1876–1957.* New York, NY: Vintage.

Cronin, T. E. (1989). *Direct democracy: The politics of initiative, referendum, and recall.* Cambridge, MA: Harvard University Press.

Crosnoe, R. (2011). *Fitting in, standing out: Navigating the social challenges of high school to get an education.* Cambridge, England: Cambridge University Press.

Crow, G. M., & Pounder, D. G. (2000, April). Interdisciplinary teacher teams: Context, design, and process. *Educational Administration Quarterly, 36*(2), 216–254.

Crowther, F., Kaagan, S. S., Ferguson, M., & Hann, L. (2002). *Developing teacher leaders: How teacher leadership enhances school success.* Thousand Oaks, CA: Corwin.

Crum, K. S., & Sherman, W. H. (2008). Facilitating high achievement: High school principals' reflections on their successful leadership practices. *Journal of Educational Administration, 46*(5), 562–580.

Csikszentmihalyi, M., & Larson, R. (1984). *Being adolescent: Conflict and growth in the teenage years.* New York, NY: Basic Books.

Cuban, L. (1988). *The managerial imperative and the practice of leadership in schools.* Albany: State University of New York Press.

Curry, M. (2008). Critical friends groups: The possibilities and limitations embedded in teacher professional communities aimed at instructional improvement and school reform. *The Teachers College Record, 110*(4), 733–774.

Dahrendorf, R. (1995). A precarious balance: Economic opportunity, civil society and political liberty. *The Responsive Community: Rights and Responsibilities, 5*(3), 13–19.

Dannetta, V. (2002). What factors influence a teacher's commitment to student learning? *Leadership and Policy in Schools, 1*(2), 144–171.

Darling-Hammond, L., Ancess, J., & Ort, S. (2002). Reinventing high school: Outcomes of the coalition campus schools project. *American Educational Research Journal, 39*(3), 639–673.

Darling-Hammond, L., & McLaughlin, M. W. (1995). Policies that support professional development in an era of reform. *Phi Delta Kappan, 76*(8), 597–604.

Datnow, A., Borman, G. D., Stringfield, S., Overman, L. T., & Castellano, M. (2003). Comprehensive school reform in culturally and linguistically diverse contexts: Implementation and outcomes from a four-year study. *Educational Evaluation and Policy Analysis, 25*(2), 143–170.

Datnow, A., & Castellano, M. E. (2001). Managing and guiding school reform: Leadership in success for all schools. *Educational Administration Quarterly, 37*(2), 219–249.

Datnow, A., Park, V., & Kennedy, B. (2008). *Acting on data: How urban high schools use data to improve instruction.* Los Angeles, CA: Center on Educational Governance.

Day, C. (2005). Sustaining success in challenging contexts: Leadership in English schools. *Journal of Educational Administration, 43*(6), 573–583.

Desimone, L. M. (2002). How can comprehensive school reform models be successfully implemented? *Review of Educational Research, 72*(3), 433–479.

Desimone, L. M., Porter, A. C., Garet, M. S., Yoon, K. S., & Birman, B. F. (2002). Effects of professional development on teachers' instruction: Results from a three-year longitudinal study. *Educational Evaluation and Policy Analysis, 24*(2), 81–112.

Dinham, S. (2005). Principal leadership for outstanding educational outcomes. *Journal of Educational Administration, 43*(4), 338–356.

Downey, D. B., von Hippel, P. T., & Broh, B. A. (2004). Are schools the great equalizer? Cognitive inequality during the summer months and the school year. *American Sociological Review, 69*(5), 613–635.

Drago-Severson, E. (2004). *Helping teachers learn: Principal leadership for adult growth and development.* Thousand Oaks, CA: Corwin.

Duffy-Hester, A. M. (1999). Teaching struggling readers in elementary school classrooms: A review of classroom reading programs and principles for instruction. *The Reading Teacher, 52*(5), 480–495.

Eckert, P. (1989). *Jocks and burnouts: Social categories and identity in the high school.* New York, NY: Teachers College Press.

Edmonds, R. (1979). Effective schools for the urban poor. *Educational Leadership, 37*(1), 15–24.

Eggert, L. L., Thompson, E. A., Herting, J. R., & Nicholas, L. J. (1995). Reducing suicide potential among high-risk youth: Tests of a school-based prevention program. *Suicide and Life-Threatening Behavior, 25*(2), 276–296.

Eilers, A. M., & Camacho, A. (2007). School culture change in the making: Leadership factors that matter. *Urban Education, 42*(6), 616–637.

Elmore, R. F. (1995). Structural reform and educational practice. *Educational Researcher, 24*(9), 23–26.

Ermeling, B. A. (2010). Tracing the effects of teacher inquiry on classroom practice. *Teaching and Teacher Education, 26*(3), 377–388.

Farrell, E. (1990). *Hanging in and dropping out: Voices of at-risk high school students.* New York, NY: Teachers College Press.

Fay, C. (1992). Empowerment through leadership: In the teachers' voice. In C. Livingston (Ed.), *Teachers as leaders: Evolving roles* (pp. 57–90). Washington, DC: National Education Association.

Felner, R., Seitsinger, A., Brand, S., Burns, A., & Bolton, N. (2007). Creating small learning communities: Lessons from the project on high-performing learning communities about "what works" in creating productive, developmentally enhancing, learning contexts. *Educational Psychologist, 42*(4), 209–221.

Finnigan, K. S., & Gross, B. (2007). Do accountability policy sanctions influence teacher motivation? Lessons from Chicago's low-performing schools. *American Educational Research Journal, 44*(3), 594–630.

Firestone, W. A., & Martinez, M. C. (2007). Districts, teacher leaders, and distributed leadership: Changing instructional practice. *Leadership and Policy in Schools, 6*(1), 3–35.

Firestone, W. A., & Wilson, B. L. (1985). Using bureaucratic and cultural linkages to improve instruction: The principal's contribution. *Educational Administration Quarterly, 21*(2), 7–30.

Flanagan, A., & Grissmer, D. (2002). The role of federal resources in closing the achievement gap. In J. E. Chubb & T. Loveless (Eds.), *Bridging the achievement gap* (pp. 199–225). Washington, DC: Brookings Institution Press.

Flutter, J., & Rudduck, J. (2004). *Consulting pupils: What's in it for schools?* London, England: Routledge.

Foster, R., & St. Hilaire, B. (2003). Leadership for school improvement: principals' and teachers perspectives. *International Electronic Journal for Leadership in Learning, 7*(3), 1–18.

Franke, M. L., Carpenter, T. P., Levi, L., & Fennema, E. (2001). Capturing teachers' generative change: A follow-up study of professional development in mathematics. *American Educational Research Journal, 38*(3), 653–689.

Freiberg, H. J., Huzinec, C. A., & Templeton, S. M. (2009). Classroom management— a pathway to student achievement: A study of fourteen inner-city elementary schools. *The Elementary School Journal, 110*(1), 63–80.

Friedkin, N. E., & Slater, M. R. (1994). School leadership and performance: A social network approach. *Sociology of Education, 67*(2), 139–157.

Fullan, M. (1982). *The meaning of educational change.* New York, NY: Teachers College Press.

Fullan, M. (1993). *Change forces: Probing the depths of educational reform.* London, England: Falmer.

Fullan, M. (2002). Leadership and sustainability. *Principal Leadership, 3*(4), 13–17.

Fullan, M., & Ballew, A. C. (2002). *Leading in a culture of change.* San Francisco, CA: Jossey-Bass.

Galletta, A., & Ayala, J. (2008). Erasure and survival: Creating a future and managing a past in a restructuring high school. *Teachers College Record, 110*(9), 1959–1985.

Gamoran, A. (1996). Effects of schooling on children and families. In A. Booth & J. Dunn (Eds.), *Family-school links: How do they affect educational outcomes?* (pp. 107–114). Mahwah, NJ: Lawrence Erlbaum Associates.

Gamoran, A. (2000). High standards: A strategy for equalizing opportunities to learn. In R. D. Kahlenberg (Ed.), *A notion at risk: Preserving public education as an engine for social mobility* (pp. 93–126). New York, NY: The Century Foundation Press.

Garet, M. S., Porter, A. C., Desimone, L., Birman, B. F., & Yoon, K. S. (2001). What makes professional development effective? Results from a national sample of teachers. *American Educational Research Journal, 38*(4), 915–945.

Gault, A., & Murphy, J. (1987, Winter). The implications of high expectations for bilingual students. *Journal of Educational Equity and Leadership, 7*(4), 301–317.

Geijsel, F., Sleegers, P., Leithwood, K., & Jantzi, D. (2003). Transformational leadership effects on teachers' commitment and effort toward school reform. *Journal of Educational Administration, 41*(3), 228–256.

Goldenberg, C. N. (2004). *Successful school change: Creating settings to improve teaching and learning.* New York, NY: Teachers College Press.

Goldring, E. B., & Pasternack, R. (1994). Principals' coordinating strategies and school effectiveness. *School Effectiveness and School Improvement, 5*(3), 239–253.

Goldstein, J. (2004). Making sense of distributed leadership: The case of peer assistance and review. *Educational Evaluation and Policy Analysis, 26*(2), 173–197.

Goodlad, J. I. (1984). *A place called school: Prospects for the future.* New York, NY: McGraw-Hill.

Gray, J., Hopkins, D., Reynolds, D., Wilcox, B., Farrell, S., & Jesson, D. (1999). *Improving schools: Performance and potential.* Philadelphia, PA: Open University Press.

Greene, J. C., & Lee, J. H. (2006). Quieting educational reform . . . with educational reform. *American Journal of Evaluation, 27*(3), 337–352.

Grissmer, D., Flanagan, A., & Williamson, S. (1998). Why did the black-white score gap narrow in the 1970s and 1980s? In C. Jencks & M. Phillips (Eds.), *The black-white test score gap* (pp. 182–226). Washington, DC: Brookings Institution Press.

Grissom, J., & Keiser, L. (2011). A supervisor like me: Race, representation, and the satisfaction and turnover decisions of public sector employees. *Journal of Policy Analysis and Management, 30*(3), 557–580.

Grissom, J., Loeb, S., & Master, B. (n.d.). *Effective instructional time use for school leaders: Longitudinal evidence from observations of principals.* Unpublished manuscript.

Gronn, P. (2009). Hybrid leadership. In K. Leithwood, B. Mascall, & T. Strauss (Eds.), *Distributed leadership according to the evidence* (pp. 17–39). London, England: Routledge.

Grossman, P., Wineburg, S., & Woolworth, S. (2001). Toward a theory of teacher community. *Teachers College Record, 103*(6), 942–1012.

Gurr, D., Drysdale, L., & Mulford, B. (2005). Successful principal leadership: Australian case studies. *Journal of Educational Administration, 43*(6), 539–551.

Gurr, D., Drysdale, L., & Mulford, B. (2006). Models of successful principal leadership. *School Leadership and Management, 26*(4), 371–395.

Guskey, T. R. (2003). Analyzing lists of the characteristics of effective professional development to promote visionary leadership. *NASSP Bulletin, 87*(637), 4–20.

Hallinan, M. T., & Kubitschek, W. N. (1999). Curriculum differentiation and high school achievement. *Social Psychology of Education, 3*(1), 41–62.

Hallinger, P., & Heck, R. (1996). Reassessing the principal's role in school effectiveness: A review of empirical research, 1980–1995. *Educational Administration Quarterly, 32*(1), 5–44.

Hallinger, P., & Heck, R. (1998). Exploring the principal's contribution to school effectiveness: 1980–1995. *School Effectiveness and School Improvement, 9*(2), 157–191.

Hallinger, P., & Murphy, J. (1985, November). Assessing the instructional management behavior of principals. *Elementary School Journal, 86*(2), 217–247.

Hallinger, P., & Murphy, J. (1986). The social context of effective schools. *American Journal of Education, 94*(3), 328–355.

Hallinger, P., & Murphy, J. (2013). Running on empty: Finding the time and capacity to lead learning. *NASSP Bulletin, 97*(1), 5–21.

Halverson, R., Grigg, J., Prichett, R., & Thomas, C. (2007). The new instructional leadership: Creating data-driven instructional systems in school. *Journal of School Leadership, 17*(2), 159–194.

Hamilton, L. S., McCaffrey, D. F., Stecher, B. M., Klein, S. P., Abby, R., & Bugliari, D. (2003). Studying large-scale reforms of instructional practice: An example from mathematics and science. *Educational Evaluation and Policy Analysis, 25*, 1–29.

Harris, A. (2003). Teacher leadership as distributed leadership: Heresy, fantasy or possibility? *School Leadership & Management, 23*(3), 313–324.

Harris, A. (2009). Distributed leadership and knowledge creation. In K. Leithwood, B. Mascall, & T. Strauss (Eds.), *Distributed leadership according to the evidence*. London, England: Routledge.

Harrison, J. W., & Lembeck, E. (1996). Emergent teacher leaders. In G. Moller & M. Katzenmeyer (Eds.), *Every teacher as a leader: Realizing the potential of teacher leadership* (pp. 101–116). San Francisco, CA: Jossey-Bass.

Hart, A. W. (1994, November). Creating teacher leadership roles. *Educational Administration Quarterly, 30*(4), 472–497.

Hart, A. W. (1995, September). Reconceiving school leadership: Emergent view. *The Elementary School Journal, 96*(1), 9–28.

Hattie, J. (2009). *Visible learning: A synthesis of over 800 meta-analyses relating to achievement.* New York, NY: Routledge.

Hawley, W. D. (1995, Summer). The false premises and false promises of the movement to private public education. *Teachers College Record, 96*(4), 735–742.

Hawley, W. D., & Valli, L. (1999). The essentials of effective professional development: A new consensus. In L. Darling-Hammond & G. Sykes (Eds.), *Teaching as the learning profession: Handbook of policy and practice* (pp. 127–150). San Francisco, CA: Jossey-Bass.

Hayes, D., Christie, P., Mills, M., & Lingard, B. (2004). Productive leaders and productive leadership: Schools as learning organisations. *Journal of Educational Administration, 42*(5), 520–538.

Heck, R. H. (1992). Principals' instructional leadership and school performance: Implications for policy development. *Educational Evaluation and Policy Analysis, 14*(1), 21–34.

Heck, R. H. (2000). Examining the impact of school quality on school outcomes and improvement: A value-added approach. *Educational Administration Quarterly, 36*(4), 513–552.

Heck, R. H., & Hallinger, P. (2009). Assessing the contribution of distributed leadership to school improvement and growth in math achievement. *American Educational Research Journal, 46*(3), 659–689.

Heck, R. H., & Hallinger, P. (n.d.). *Assessing the contribution of principal and collaborative leadership.* Unpublished manuscript.

Heller, M. F., & Firestone, W. A. (1995). Who's in charge here? Sources of leadership for change in eight schools. *The Elementary School Journal, 96*(1), 65–86.

Herbst, J. (1996). *The once and future school: Three hundred and fifty years of American secondary education.* New York, NY: Routledge.

Heyns, B. (1974). Social selection and stratification within schools. *American Journal of Sociology, 79*(6), 1434–1451.

Hiebert, E. H., & Pearson, P. D. (1999). *Building on the past, bridging to the future: A research agenda for the Center for the Improvement of Early Reading Achievement.* Ann Arbor: University of Michigan, Center for the Improvement of Early Reading Achievement.

Hill, H. C., Rowan, B., & Ball, D. L. (2005). Effects of teachers' mathematical knowledge for teaching on student achievement. *American Educational Research Journal, 42*(2), 371–406.

Horn, I. S. (2005). Learning on the job: A situated account of teacher learning in high school mathematics departments. *Cognition and Instruction, 23*(2), 207–236.

Horn, I. S. (2010). Teaching replays, teaching rehearsals, and re-visions of practice: Learning from colleagues in a mathematics teacher community. *Teachers College Record, 112*(1), 225–259.

Hoy, W., Hannum, J., & Tschannen-Moran, M. (1998). Organizational climate and student achievement: A parsimonious and longitudinal view. *Journal of School Leadership, 8*(4), 336–359.

Huberman, M., Parrish, T., Hannan, S., Arellanes, M., & Shambaugh, L. (2011). *Turnaround schools in California: Who are they and what strategies do they use?* San Francisco, CA: WestEd.

Ingram, D., Seashore Louis, K., & Schroeder, R. (2004). Accountability policies and teacher decision making: Barriers to the use of data to improve practice. *Teachers College Record, 106*(6), 1258–1287.

Irvine, J. J. (1990). *Black students and school failure: Policies, practices, and prescriptions.* New York, NY: Greenwood.

Jackson, D. S. (2000). The school improvement journey: Perspectives on leadership. *School Leadership and Management, 20*(1), 61–78.

Johnson Jr., J. F., & Asera, R. (1999). *Hope for urban education: A study of nine high-performing, high-poverty, urban elementary schools.* Washington, DC: U.S. Department of Education, Planning and Evaluation Services.

Jordan, W., & Cooper, R. (2003). High school reform and black male students: Limits and possibilities of policy and practice. *Urban Education, 38*(2), 196–216.

Joselowsky, F. (2007). Youth engagement, high school reform, and improved learning outcomes: Building systemic approaches for youth engagement. *NASSP Bulletin, 91*(3), 253–276.

Judge, T. A., Bono, J. E., Ilies, R., & Gerhardt, M. W. (2002). Personality and leadership: A qualitative and quantitative review. *Journal of Applied Psychology, 87*(4), 765–780.

Katzenmeyer, M., & Moller, G. (2001). *Awakening the sleeping giant: Helping teachers develop as leaders.* Newbury Park, CA: Corwin.

Kerr, K., Marsh, J., Ikemoto, G., Darilek, H., & Barney, H. (2006). Strategies to promote data use for instructional improvement actions, outcomes, and lessons from three urban districts. *American Journal of Education, 112*(4), 496–520.

Kilcher, A. (1992). Becoming a change facilitator: The first-year experience of five teacher leaders. In C. Livingston (Ed.), *Teachers as leaders: Evolving roles* (pp. 91–113). Washington, DC: National Education Association.

Killion, J. P. (1996). Moving beyond the school: Teacher leaders in the district office. In G. Moller & M. Katzenmeyer (Eds.), *Every teacher as a leader: Realizing the potential of teacher leadership* (pp. 63–84). San Francisco: Jossey-Bass.

King, M. (2001). Professional development to promote schoolwide inquiry. *Teaching and Teacher Education, 18*(3), 243–257.

Klecker, B. J., & Loadman, W. E. (1998, Spring). Defining and measuring the dimensions of teacher empowerment in restructuring public schools. *Education, 118*(3), 358–371.

Kleiner, B., & Lewis, L. (2005). *Dual enrollment of high school students at postsecondary institutions: 2002–03.* (NCES 2005-008). Washington, DC: National Center for Education Statistics, U.S. Department of Education.

Kleinfeld, J. (1975). Effective teachers of Eskimo and Indian students. *The School Review, 83*(2), 301–344.

Kliebard, H. M. (1995). *The struggle for the American curriculum 1893–1958* (2nd ed.). New York, NY: Routledge.

Kober, N. (2001, April). *It takes more than testing: Closing the achievement.* A report of the Center on Education Policy. Washington, DC: Center on Education Policy.

Kochanek, J. R. (2005). *Building trust for better schools: Research-based practices.* Thousand Oaks, CA: Corwin.

Koos, L. (1927). *The American secondary school.* Boston, MA: Ginn.

Krug, E. A. (1964). *The shaping of the American high school.* New York, NY: Harper & Row.

Kruse, S., Seashore Louis, K., & Bryk, A. (1995). An emerging framework for analyzing school-based professional community. In K. Seashore Louis & S. Kruse (Eds.), *Professionalism and community: Perspectives on reforming urban schools* (pp. 23–44). Thousand Oaks, CA: Corwin.

Lachat, M. A., & Smith, S. (2005). Practices that support data use in urban high schools. *Journal of Education for Students Placed at Risk, 10*(3), 333–349.

Laffey, J. (1982). The assessment of involvement with school work among urban high school students. *Journal of Educational Psychology, 74*(1), 62–71.

Land, D., & Legters, N. (2002). The extent and consequences of risk in U.S. education. In S. Stringfield & D. Land (Eds.), *Educating at-risk students. 101st yearbook of the National Society for the Study of Education. Part II* (pp. 1–28). Chicago, IL: The University of Chicago Press.

LeBlanc, P. R., & Shelton, M. M. (1997, Fall). Teacher leadership: The needs of teachers. *Action in Teacher Education, 19*(3), 32–48.

Lee, V. E., & Burkam, D. T. (2003). Dropping out of high school: The role of school organization and structure. *American Educational Research Journal, 40*(2), 353–393.

Leithwood, K. (2005). Understanding successful principal leadership: Progress on a broken front. *Journal of Educational Administration, 43*(6), 619–629.

Leithwood, K. (2006). *Teacher working conditions that matter: Evidence for change.* Ontario, Canada: Elementary Teachers' Federation of Ontario.

Leithwood, K. (2008). *School leadership, evidence-based decision making and large-scale student assessment.* Paper presented at International Perspectives on Student Assessment Lecture Series, University of Calgary, Alberta, Canada.

Leithwood, K. (2011). School leadership, evidence-based decision making, and large-scale student assessment. In C. F. Weber & J. L. Lupart (Eds.), *Leading student assessment* (pp. 17–39). New York, NY: Weber.

Leithwood, K., Anderson, S., Mascall, B., & Strauss, T. (2011). School leaders' influences on student learning: The four paths. In T. Bush, L. Bell, & D. Middlewood (Eds.), *The principles of educational leadership and management* (pp. 13–30). Thousand Oaks, CA: SAGE.

Leithwood, K., Day, C., Sammons, P., Harris, A., & Hopkins, D. (2006). *Successful school leadership. What it is and how it influences pupil learning.* London, England: Department of Education and Skills.

Leithwood, K., & Jantzi, D. (2000). The effects of transformational leadership on organizational conditions and student engagement with school. *Journal of Educational Administration, 38*(2), 112–129.

Leithwood, K., & Jantzi, D. (2005). A review of transformational school leadership research 1996–2005. *Leadership and Policy in Schools, 4*(3), 177–199.

Leithwood, K., & Jantzi, D. (2006). Transformational school leadership for large-scale reform: Effects on students, teachers, and their classroom practices. *School Effectiveness and School Improvement, 17*(2), 201–227.

Leithwood, K., Jantzi, D., & Steinbach, R. (1999). *Changing leadership for changing times.* Philadelphia, PA: Open University Press.

Leithwood, K. A. & Montgomery, D.J. (1982). The role of the elementary principal in program improvement. *Review of Educational Research, 52*(3), 309–339.

Leithwood, K., Patten, S., & Jantzi, D. (2010). Testing a conception of how school leadership influences student learning. *Educational Administration Quarterly, 46*(5), 671–706.

Leithwood, K., Seashore Louis, K., Anderson, S., & Wahlstrom, K. (2004). *Review of research: How leadership influences student learning.* New York, NY: The Wallace Foundation, Center for Applied Research and Educational Improvement and Ontario Institute for Studies in Education.

Leitner, D. (1994). Do principals affect student outcomes: An organizational perspective. *School Effectiveness and School Improvement, 5*(3), 219–238.

Levin, J. A., & Datnow, A. (2012). The principal role in data-driven decision making: Using case-study data to develop multi-mediator models of educational reform. *School Effectiveness and School Improvement, 23*(2), 179–201.

Levine, T. H., & Marcus, A. S. (2007). Closing the achievement gap through teacher collaboration: Facilitating multiple trajectories of teacher learning. *Journal of Advanced Academics, 19*(1), 116–138.

Levine, T. H., & Marcus, A. S. (2010). How the structure and focus of teachers' collaborative activities facilitate and constrain teacher learning. *Teaching and Teacher Education, 26*(3), 389–398.

Lieberman, A., & Miller, L. (1999). *Teachers—transforming their world and their work.* New York, NY: Teachers College Press.

Little, J. W. (1982). Norms of collegiality and experimentation: Workplace conditions of school success. *American Educational Research Journal, 19*(3), 325–340.

Little, J. W. (1985, November). Teachers as teacher advisors: The delicacy of collegial leadership. *Educational Leadership, 43*(3), 34–36.

Little, J. W. (1987). Teachers as colleagues. In V. Richardson-Koehler (Ed.), *Educators' handbook: A research perspective* (pp. 491–518). White Plains, NY: Longman.

Little, J. W. (1988). Assessing the prospects for teacher leadership. In A. Lieberman (Ed.), *Building a professional culture in schools* (pp. 78–105). New York, NY: Teachers College Press.

Littrell, P. C., Billingsley, B. S., & Cross, L. H. (1994). The effects of principal support on special and general educators' stress, job satisfaction, school commitment, health, and intent to stay in teaching. *Remedial and Special Education, 15*(5), 297–310.

Lomotey, K. (1989). *African-American principals: School leadership and success.* New York, NY: Greenwood Press.

Louis, K. S. (2007). Trust and improvement in schools. *Journal of Educational Change, 8*(1), 1–24.

Louis, K. S., Dretzke, B., & Wahlstrom, K. (2010, Sept). How does leadership affect student achievement? Results from a national US survey. *School Effectiveness and School Improvement, 21*(3), 315–336.

Louis, K. S., & Marks, H. M. (1998). Does professional community affect the classroom? Teachers' work and student work in restructuring schools. *American Journal of Education, 106*(4), 532–575.

Louis, K. S., Marks, H. M., & Kruse, S. (1996). Teachers' professional community in restructuring schools. *American Educational Research Journal, 33*(4), 757–798.

Louis, K. S., & Miles, M. B. (1990). *Improving the urban high school: What works and why.* New York, NY: Teachers College Press.

Louis, K. S., & Miles, M. B. (1991). Managing reform: Lessons from urban high schools. *School effectiveness and school improvement, 2*(2), 75–96.

Lucas, S. R., & Gamoran, A. (2002). Tracking and the achievement gap. In J. E. Chubb & T. Loveless (Eds.), *Bridging the achievement gap* (pp. 171–198). Washington, DC: Brookings Institution Press.

Lynch, M., & Strodl, P. (1991). *Teacher leadership: Preliminary development of a questionnaire.* Paper presented at the annual conference of the Eastern Educational Research Association, Boston, MA.

Lyons, C. A., & Pinnell, G. S. (1999). Teacher development: The best investment in literacy education. In J. S. Gaffney & B. J. Askew (Eds.). *Stirring the waters: The influence of Marie Clay* (pp. 197–220). Portsmouth, NH: Heinemann.

MacBeath, J. (2009). Distributed leadership: Paradigms, policy, and paradox. In K. Leithwood, B. Mascall, & T. Strauss (Eds.), *Distributed leadership according to the evidence* (pp. 41–57). London, England: Routledge.

Malen, B., & Rice, J. K. (2004). A framework for assessing the impact of education reforms on school capacity: Insights from studies of high-stakes accountability initiatives. *Educational Policy, 18*(5), 631–660.

Mangin, M. M. (2007). Facilitating elementary principals' support for instructional teacher leadership. *Educational Administration Quarterly, 43*(3), 319–357.

Manning, J. C. (1995). Ariston metron. *The Reading Teacher, 48*(8), 650–659.

Manthei, J. (1992). *The mentor teacher as leader: The motives, characteristics and needs of seventy-three experienced teachers who seek a new leadership role.* Paper presented at the Annual Meeting of the American Educational Research Association, San Francisco, CA. ERIC Document Reproduction Service No ED 346042.

Marks, H. M. (2000). Student engagement in instructional activity: Patterns in the elementary, middle, and high school years. *American Educational Research Journal, 37*(1), 153–184.

Marzano, R. J., Waters, T., & McNulty, B. A. (2005). *School leadership that works: From research to results.* Alexandria, VA: Association for Supervision and Curriculum Development.

May, H., & Supovitz, J. A. (2011). The scope of principal efforts to improve instruction. *Educational Administration Quarterly, 47*(2), 332–352.

Mayrowetz, D., Murphy, J., Seashore Louis, K., & Smylie, M. (2009). Conceptualizing distributed leadership as a school reform. In K. Leithwood, B. Mascall, & T. Strauss (Eds.), *Distributed leadership according to the evidence* (pp. 167–195). London, England: Routledge.

Mayrowetz, D., & Weinstein, C. S. (1999). Sources of leadership for inclusive education: Creating schools for all children. *Educational Administration Quarterly, 35*(3), 423–449.

McDougall, D., Saunders, W. M., & Goldenberg, C. (2007). Inside the black box of school reform: Explaining the how and why of change at Getting Results schools. *International Journal of Disability, Development and Education, 54*(1), 51–89.

McLaughlin, M. W., & Talbert, J. E. (2001). *Professional communities and the work of high school teaching.* Chicago, IL: University of Chicago Press.

Mickelson, R. A., & Heath, D. (1999). The effects of segregation and tracking on African American high school seniors' academic achievement. *Journal of Negro Education, 68*(4), 566–586.

Miller, L. S. (1995). *An American imperative: Accelerating minority educational advancement.* New Haven, CT: Yale University Press.

Mitchell, C., & Castle, J. B. (2005). The instructional role of elementary school principals. *Canadian Journal of Education/Revue Canadienne de l'education, 3*(28), 409–433.

Mitchell, C., & Sackney, L. (2006). Building schools, building people: The school principal's role in leading a learning community. *Journal of School Leadership, 16*(5), 627–640.

Moller, G., & Katzenmeyer, M. (1996). The promise of teacher leadership. In G. Moller & M. Katzenmeyer (Eds.), *Every teacher as a leader: Realizing the potential of teacher leadership* (pp. 1–18). San Francisco, CA: Jossey-Bass.

Moller, J., & Eggen, A. B. (2005). Team leadership in upper secondary education. *School Leadership and Management, 25*(4), 331–347.

Morrissey, M. S. (2000). *Professional learning communities: An ongoing exploration.* Austin, TX: Southwest Educational Development Laboratory.

Mukuria, G. (2002). Disciplinary challenges. *Urban Education, 37*(3), 432–452.

Mulford, B., & Silins, H. (2003). Leadership for organisational learning and improved student outcomes—what do we know. *Cambridge Journal of Education, 33*(2), 175–195.

Mullen, C. A., & Hutinger, J. L. (2008). The principal's role in fostering collaborative learning communities through faculty study group development. *Theory into Practice, 47*(4), 276–285.

Murphy, J. (1988, Spring). Equity as student opportunity to learn: Findings and implications. *Theory into Practice, 27*(2), 145–151.

Murphy, J. (1990a, April). Instructional leadership: Focus on curriculum responsibilities. *NASSP Bulletin, 74*(525), 1–4.

Murphy, J. (1990b). Principal instructional leadership. In L. S. Lotto & P. W. Thurston (Eds.), *Advances in educational administration: Changing perspectives on the school.* (Volume 1, Part B). Greenwich, CT: JAI Press.

Murphy, J. (1991). *Restructuring schools: Capturing and assessing the phenomena.* New York, NY: Teachers College Press.

Murphy, J. (1992). School effectiveness and school restructuring: Contributions to educational improvement. *School Effectiveness and School Improvement, 3*(2), 90–109.

Murphy, J. (2002, April). Reculturing the profession of educational leadership: New blueprints. *Educational Administration Quarterly, 38*(3), 176–191.

Murphy, J. (2005). *Connecting teacher leadership and school improvement.* Thousand Oaks, CA: Corwin.

Murphy, J. (2010). *The educator's handbook for understanding and closing achievement gaps.* Thousand Oaks, CA: Corwin.

Murphy, J. (2013a). The architecture of school improvement. *Journal of Educational Administration, 51*(3), 252–263.

Murphy, J. (2013b). *The architecture of school improvement: Lessons learned.* Thousand Oaks, CA: Corwin.

Murphy, J. (2015). Creating communities of professionalism: Addressing cultural and structural barriers. *Journal of Educational Administration 53* (2), p. 154–176.

Murphy, J., Beck, L. G., Crawford, M., & Hodges, A. (2001). *The productive high school: Creating personalized academic communities.* Thousand Oaks, CA: Corwin.

Murphy, J., Elliott, S. N., Goldring, E., & Porter, A. (2007, April). Leadership for learning: A research-based model and taxonomy of behaviors. *School Leadership & Management, 27*(2), 179–201.

Murphy, J., & Hallinger, P. (1989). Equity as access to learning: Curriculum and instructional treatment differences. *Journal of Curriculum Studies, 2*(21), 129–149.

Murphy, J., Hallinger, P., & Lotto, L. S. (1986, November–December). Inequitable allocations of alterable learning variables in schools and classrooms. *Journal of Teacher Education, 37*(6), 21–26.

Murphy, J., Hallinger, P., & Mesa, R. P. (1985). School effectiveness: Checking progress and assumptions and developing a role for state and federal government. *Teachers College Record, 86*(4), 615–641.

Murphy, J., Hallinger, P., Weil, M., & Mitman, A. (1983). Instructional leadership: A conceptual framework. *Planning and Changing, 14*(3), 136–149.

Murphy, J., Hull, T., & Walker, A. (1987, July/August). Academic drift and curricular debris: An analysis of high school course-taking patterns with implications for local policy makers. *Journal of Curriculum Studies, 19*(4), 341–360.

Murphy, J., & Torre, D. (2014). *Creating productive cultures in schools: For students, teachers, and parents.* Thousand Oaks, CA: Corwin.

Murphy, J., Weil, M., Hallinger, P., & Mitman, A. (1982, December). Academic press: Translating high expectations into school policies and classroom practices. *Educational Leadership, 40*(3), 22–26.

Murphy, J., Weil, M., Hallinger, P., & Mitman, A. (1985, Spring). School effectiveness: A conceptual framework. *The Educational Forum, 49*(3), 361–374.

Murtadha, K. (2009). Notes from the (battle) field for equity in education. *Leadership and Policy in Schools, 8*(3), 342–354.

Nelson, B. S., & Sassi, A. (2005). *The effective principal: Institutional leadership in high quality learning.* New York, NY: Teachers College Press.

Newmann, F. M. (1992). Conclusion. In F. M. Newmann (Ed.), *Student engagement and achievement in American secondary schools* (pp. 182–217). New York, NY: Teachers College Record.

Newmann, F. M., King, M. B., & Youngs, P. (2000). Professional development that addresses school capacity: Lessons from urban elementary schools. *American Journal of Education, 108*(4), 259–299.

Newmann, F. M., Smith, B., Allensworth, E., & Bryk, A. S. (2001). Instructional program coherence: What it is and why it should guide school improvement policy. *Educational Evaluation and Policy Analysis, 23*(4), 297–321.

Newmann, F. M., Wehlage, G. G., & Lamburn, S. D. (1992). The significance and sources of student engagement. In F. M. Newmann (Ed.), *Student engagement and achievement in American secondary schools* (pp. 11–39). New York, NY: Teachers College Press.

Noguera, P. (1996). Responding to the crisis confronting California's black male youth: Providing support without furthering marginalization. *The Journal of Negro Education, 65*(2), 219–236.

Nye, B., Konstantopoulos, S., & Hedges, L. V. (2004). How large are teacher effects? *Educational Evaluation and Policy Analysis, 26*(3), 237–257.

Oakes, J. (1985). *Keeping track: How schools structure inequality.* New Haven, CT: Yale University Press.

Oakes, J., & Guiton, G. (1995). Matchmaking: The dynamics of high school tracking decisions. *American Educational Research Journal, 32*(1), 3–33.

O'Donnell, R. J., & White, G. P. (2005). Within the accountability era: Principals' instructional leadership behaviors and student achievement. *NASSP Bulletin, 89*(645), 56–71.

Olivier, D., & Hipp, K. K. (2006). Leadership capacity and collective efficacy: Interacting to sustain student learning in a professional learning community. *Journal of School Leadership, 16*(5), 505–519.

Owen, S. (2003). School-based professional development: Building morale, professionalism and productive teacher learning practices. *The Journal of Educational Enquiry, 2*(4), 102–128.

Palincsar, A., Magnusson, S., Marano, N., Ford, D., & Brown, N. (1998). Designing a community of practice: Principles and practices of the GIsML (Guided Inquiry supporting Multiple Literacies) community. *Teaching and Teacher Education, 14*(1), 5–19.

Patterson, N., Beltyukova, S., Berman, K., & Francis, A. (2007). The making of sophomores: Student, parent, and teacher reactions in the context of systemic urban high school reform. *Urban Education, 42*(2), 124–144.

Patty, D., Maschoff, J. D., & Ranson, P. E. (1996). *The reading resource handbook for school leaders.* Norwood, MA: Christopher-Gordon.

Penuel, W. R., Fishman, B. J., Yamaguchi, R., & Gallagher, L. P. (2007). What makes professional development effective? Strategies that foster curriculum implementation. *American Educational Research Journal, 44*(4), 921–958.

Penuel, W. R., Frank, K. A., & Krause, A. (2006). *The distribution of resources and expertise and the implementation of schoolwide reform initiatives.* In S. A. Barab, K. E. Hay, & D. T. Hickey (Eds.), Proceedings of the 7th International Conference of the Learning Sciences (Vol. 1, pp. 522–528). Mahwah, NJ: Lawrence Erlbaum Associates.

Penuel, W. R., Riel, M., Joshi, A., Pearlman, L., Kim, C. M., & Frank, K. A. (2010). The alignment of the informal and formal organizational supports for reform: Implications for improving teaching in schools. *Educational Administration Quarterly, 46*(1), 57–95.

Penuel, W. R., Riel, M., Krause, A., & Frank, K. (2009). Analyzing teachers' professional interactions in a school as social capital: A social network approach. *The Teachers College Record, 111*(1), 124–163.

Phillips, J. (2003). Powerful learning: Creating learning communities in urban school reform. *Journal of Curriculum and Supervision, 18*(3), 240–258.

Pinnell, G. S., Lyons, C. A., DeFord, D. E., Bryk, A. S., & Seltzer, M. (1994). Comparing instructional models for the literacy education of high-risk first graders. *Reading Research Quarterly, 29*(1), 9–39.

Porter, A. C., Garet, M. S., Desimone, L. M., & Birman, B. F. (2003). Providing effective professional development: Lessons from the Eisenhower Program. *Science Educator, 12*(1), 23–40.

Pounder, D. G. (1999). Teacher teams: Exploring job characteristics and work-related outcomes of work group enhancement. *Educational Administration Quarterly, 35*(3), 317–348.

Powell, A. G., Farrar, E., & Cohen, D. K. (1985). *The shopping mall high school: Winners and losers in the educational marketplace.* Boston, MA: Houghton-Mifflin.

Prawat, R. S., & Peterson, P. L. (1999). Social constructivist views of learning. In J. Murphy & K. S. Louis (Eds.), *Handbook of research on educational administration* (2nd ed., pp. 203–226). San Francisco, CA: Jossey-Bass.

Prestine, N. A. (1995). Crisscrossing the landscape: Another turn at cognition and educational administration. *Educational Administration Quarterly, 31*(1), 134–142.

Printy, S. M. (2008). Leadership for teacher learning: A community of practice perspective. *Educational Administration Quarterly, 44*(2), 187–226.

Putnam, R. D. (1995). Bowling alone: America's declining social capital. *Journal of Democracy, 6*(1), 65–77.

Quint, J. (2006). *Meeting five critical challenges of high school reform: Lessons from research on three reform models.* New York, NY: Manpower Demonstration Research Corporation.

Quiroz, P. A. (2001). The silencing of Latino student "voice": Puerto Rican and Mexican narratives in eighth grade and high school. *Anthropology & Education Quarterly, 32*(3), 326–349.

Raywid, M. (1995). Professional community and its yield at Metro Academy. In K. S. Louis & S. Kruse (Eds.), *Professionalism and community: Perspectives on reforming urban schools* (pp. 43–75). Thousand Oaks, CA: Corwin.

Riehl, C., & Sipple, J. (1996). Making the most of time and talent: Secondary school organizational climates, teaching task environments, and teacher commitment. *American Educational Research Journal, 33*(4), 873–901.

Riester, A. F., Pursch, V., & Skria, L. (2002). Principals for social justice: Leaders of school success for children from low-income homes. *Journal of School Leadership, 12*(3), 281–304.

Robinson, V. M. J. (2007). *School leadership and student outcomes: Identifying what works and why.* Sydney, NSW: Australian Council for Educational Leaders.

Robinson, V. M. J. (2008). Forging the links between distributed leadership and educational outcomes. *Journal of Educational Administration, 46*(2), 241–256.

Robinson, V. M. J., Lloyd, C. A., & Rowe, K. J. (2008). The impact of leadership on student outcomes: An analysis of the differential effects of leadership types. *Educational Administration Quarterly, 44*(5), 635–674.

Rodríguez, L. (2008). Teachers know you can do more: Understanding how school cultures of success affect urban high school students. *Educational Policy, 22*(5), 758–780.

Roney, K., Coleman, H., & Schlichting, K. A. (2007). Linking the organizational health of middle grades schools to student achievement. *NASSP Bulletin, 91*(4), 289–321.

Roscigno, V. J. (1998, March). Race and the reproduction of educational disadvantage. *Social Forces, 76*(3), 1033–1061.

Roscigno, V. J. (1999). The black-white achievement gap, family-school links, and the importance of place. *Sociological Inquiry, 69*(2), 159–186.

Ross, S., Sterbinsky, A., & McDonald, A. (2003). *School variables as determinants of the success of comprehensive school reform: A quantitative study of 69 inner-city schools.* Paper presented to American Educational Research Association, Chicago, IL.

Rossmiller, R. A. (1992). The secondary school principal and teachers' quality of work life. *Educational Management Administration & Leadership, 20*(3), 132–146.

Rowan, B., & Miller, R. J. (2007). Organizational strategies for promoting instructional change: Implementation dynamics in schools working with comprehensive school reform providers. *American Educational Research Journal, 44*(2), 252–297.

Rowe, K. J. (1995). Factors affecting students' progress in reading: Key findings from a longitudinal study. *Literacy, Teaching and Learning, 1*(2), 57–110.

Rudduck, J., Chaplain, R., & Wallace, G. (1996). *School improvement: What can pupils tell us?* London, England: Routledge.

Rumberger, R. W. (2011). *Dropping out: Why students drop out of high school and what can be done about it.* Cambridge, MA: Harvard University Press.

Rumberger, R. W., & Palardy, G. J. (2005, September). Does segregation still matter? The impact of student composition on academic achievement in high school. *Teachers College Record, 107*(9), 1999–2043.

Rutter, M. (1983, February). School effects on pupil progress: Research findings and policy implications. *Child Development, 54*(1), 1–29.

Samuels. S. J. (1981). Characteristics of exemplary reading programs. In J. T. Guthrie (Ed.), *Comprehension and teaching: Research review* (pp. 255–273). Newark, DE: International Reading Association.

Sarason, S. B. (1994). *Parental involvement and the political principle: Why the existing governance structure of schools should be abolished.* San Francisco, CA: Jossey-Bass.

Sather, S. E. (1999). Leading, lauding, and learning: Leadership in secondary schools serving diverse populations. *Journal of Negro Education, 68*(4), 511–528.

Saunders, W. M., Goldenberg, C. N., & Gallimore, R. (2009). Increasing achievement by focusing grade-level teams on improving classroom learning: A prospective, quasi-experimental study of Title I schools. *American Educational Research Journal, 46*(4), 1006–1033.

Scanlan, M., & Lopez, F. (2012). Vamos! How school leaders promote equity and excellence for bilingual students. *Educational Administration Quarterly, 48*(4), 583–625.

Scheerens, J. (1997). Conceptual models and theory-embedded principles on effective schooling. *School Effectiveness and School Improvement, 8*(3), 269–310.

Scribner, J. P., Cockrell, K. S., Cockrell, D. H., & Valentine, J. W. (1999). Creating professional communities in schools through organizational learning: An evaluation of a school improvement process. *Educational Administration Quarterly, 35*(1), 130–160.

Sebastian, J., & Allensworth, E. (2012). The influence of principal leadership on classroom instruction and student learning: A study of mediated pathways to learning. *Educational Administration Quarterly, 48*(4), 626–663.

Sergiovanni, T. J. (1991a). The dark side of professionalism in educational administration. *Phi Delta Kappan, 72*(7), 521–526.

Sergiovanni, T. J. (1991b). *The principalship: A reflective practice perspective* (2nd ed.). Boston, MA: Allyn & Bacon.

Shannon, S. G., & Bylsma, P. (2002, November). *Addressing the achievement gap: A challenge for Washington state educators.* Olympia, WA: Washington Office of the State Superintendent of Public Instruction. (ED 474 392)

Shear, L., Means, B., Mitchell, K., House, A., Gorges, T., Joshi, A., . . . Shlonik, J. (2008). Contrasting paths to small-school reform: Results of a 5-year evaluation of the Bill & Melinda Gates Foundation's National High Schools Initiative. *Teachers College Record, 110*(9), 1986–2039.

Shouse, R. (1996). Academic press and sense of community: Conflict, congruence, and implications for student achievement. *Social Psychology of Education, 1*(1), 47–68.

Silins, H., & Mulford, B. (2004). Schools as learning organisations: Effects on teacher leadership and student outcomes. *School Effectiveness and School Improvement, 3*(4), 443–466.

Silins, H., & Mulford, B. (2010). Re-conceptualising school principalship that improves student outcomes. *Journal of Educational Leadership, Policy and Practice, 25*(2), 74–93.

Singham, M. (2003, April). The achievement gap: Myths and reality. *Phi Delta Kappan, 84*(8), 586–591.

Siskin, L. S. (1994). *Realms of knowledge: Academic departments in secondary schools.* Washington, DC: Falmer.

Sizer, T. R. (1964). *Secondary schools at the turn of the century.* New Haven, CT: Yale University Press.

Smerdon, B. A., & Borman, K. M. (2009). Secondary school reform. In B. A. Smerdon & K. M. Borman (Eds.), *Saving America's high schools* (pp. 1–17). Washington, DC: The Urban Institute Press.

Smerdon, B. A., Borman, K. M., & Hannaway, J. (2009). Conclusions: Implications for future reform efforts, research, and policy. In B. A. Smerdon & K. M. Borman (Eds.), *Saving America's high schools* (pp. 201–215). Washington, DC: The Urban Institute Press.

Smylie, M. A., Conley, S., & Marks, H. M. (2002). Exploring new approaches to teacher leadership for school improvement. In J. Murphy (Ed.), *The educational leadership challenge: Redefining leadership for the 21st century* (pp. 162–188). Chicago, IL: University of Chicago Press.

Smylie, M. A., & Hart, A. W. (1999). School leadership for teacher learning: A human and social capital development perspective. In J. Murphy & K. S. Louis, *Handbook of research on educational administration* (2nd ed., pp. 421–441). San Francisco, CA: Jossey-Bass.

Southworth, G. (2002). Instructional leadership in schools: Reflections and empirical evidence. *School Leadership & Management, 22*(1), 73–91.

Spears, H. (1941). *Secondary education in American life.* New York, NY: American Book.

Spillane, J. P., Diamond, J. B., Walker, L. J., Halverson, R., & Jita, L. (2001). Urban school leadership for elementary science instruction: Identifying and activating resources in an undervalued school subject. *Journal of Research in Science Teaching, 38*(8), 918–940.

Spring, J. (1990). *The American school 1642–1990: Varieties of historical interpretation of the foundations and developments of American education* (2nd ed.). New York, NY: Longman.

Steele, C. M. (1997). A threat in the air: How stereotypes shape the intellectual identities and performances of women and African Americans. *American Psychologist, 52*(6), 613–629.

Stein, M. K., & Coburn, C. E. (2008). Architectures for learning: A comparative analysis of two urban school districts. *American Journal of Education, 114*(4), 583–626.

Stiggins, R., & Chappuis, J. (2006). Using student-involved classroom assessment to close achievement gaps. *Theory into Practice, 44*(1), 11–18.

Stigler, J. W., & Hiebert, J. (1999). *The teaching gap: Best ideas from the world's teachers for improving education in the classroom.* New York, NY: The Free Press.

Stoll, L., Bolam, R., McMahon, A., Wallace, M., & Thomas, S. (2006). Professional learning communities: A review of the literature. *Journal of Educational Change, 7*(4), 221–258.

Strahan, D. (2003). Promoting a collaborative professional culture in three elementary schools that have beaten the odds. *The Elementary School Journal, 104*(2), 127–146.

Stringfield, S., & Reynolds, D. (2012). *Creating and sustaining secondary schools success at scale—Sandfields, Cwmtawe, and the Neath-port Talbot local education authority's high reliability schools reform.* Paper presented at the National Conference on Scaling Up Effective Schools, Nashville, TN.

Strutchens, M. E., & Silver, E. A. (2000). NAEP findings regarding race/ethnicity: Students' performance, school experiences, and attitudes and beliefs. In E. A. Silver & P. A. Kenney (Eds.), *Results from the seventh mathematics assessment of the National Assessment of Educational Progress* (pp. 45–72). Reston, VA: National Council of Teachers of Mathematics.

Supovitz, J. (2002). Developing communities of instructional practice. *The Teachers College Record, 104*(8), 1591–1626.

Supovitz, J. (2008). Instructional influence in American high schools. In M. M. Mangin, & S. R. Stoelinga (Eds.), *Effective teacher leadership: Using research to inform and reform* (pp. 144–162). New York, NY: Teachers College Press.

Supovitz, J. (2010). Is high-stakes testing working? *A Review of Research, 7*(2). Retrieved July 2, 2015, from http://www.gse.upenn.edu/review/feature/supovitz

Supovitz, J. A., & Christman, J. B. (2003). *Developing communities of instructional practice: Lessons from Cincinnati and Philadelphia.* Philadelphia: Consortium for Policy Research in Education, University of Pennsylvania.

Supovitz, J. A., & Klein, V. (2003). *Mapping a course for improved student learning: How innovative schools systematically use student performance data to guide improvement.* Philadelphia, PA: Consortium for Policy Research in Education.

Supovitz, J. A., & Poglinco, S. M. (2001). *Instructional leadership in a standards-based reform.* Philadelphia, PA: Consortium for Policy Research in Education.

Supovitz, J., Sirinides, P., & May, H. (2010). How principals and peers influence teaching and learning. *Educational Administration Quarterly, 46*(1), 31–56.

Supovitz, J. A., & Turner, H. M. (2000). The effects of professional development on science teaching practices and classroom culture. *Journal of Research in Science Teaching, 37*(9), 963–980.

Sweeney, J. (1982). Research synthesis on effective school leadership. *Educational Leadership, 39*(5), 346–352.

Tate, W. F. (1997). Race-ethnicity, SES, gender, and language proficiency trends in mathematics achievement: An update. *Journal for Research in Mathematics Education, 28*(6), 652–679.

Thompson, C. L. (2002). *Research-based review of reports on closing achievement gaps: Report to the education cabinet and the joint legislative oversight committee.* Chapel Hill: The North Carolina Education Research Council.

Thompson, C. L., & O'Quinn III, S. D. (2001). *Eliminating the black-white achievement gap: A summary of research.* Chapel Hill: North Carolina Education Research Council.

Tichy, N. M., & Cardwell, N. (2004). *The cycle of leadership: How great leaders teach their companies to win.* New York, NY: Harper Business.

Timperley, H. (2009). Distributed leadership to improve outcomes for students. In K. Leithwood, B. Mascall, & T. Strauss (Eds.), *Distributed leadership according to the evidence* (pp. 197–222). London, England: Routledge.

Tushman, M. L., & Romanelli, E. (1985). Organizational evolution: A metamorphosis model of convergence and reorientation. In L. L. Cummings & B. M. Straw (Eds.), *Research in organizational behavior* (pp. 171–222). Greenwich, CT: JAI Press.

Tyack, D. B. (1974). *The one best system: A history of American urban education.* Cambridge, MA: Harvard University Press.

Tyack, D. B. (1993). School governance in the United States: Historical puzzles and anomalies. In J. Hannaway & M. Carnoy (Eds.), *Decentralization and school improvement* (pp. 1–32). San Francisco, CA: Jossey-Bass.

Useem, E. L., Christman, J. B., Gold, E., & Simon, E. (1997). Reforming alone: Barriers to organizational learning in urban school change initiatives. *Journal of Education for Students Placed at Risk (JESPAR), 2*(1), 55–78.

Vescio, V., Ross, D., & Adams, A. (2008). A review of research on the impact of professional learning communities on teaching practice and student learning. *Teaching and Teacher Education, 24*(1), 80–91.

Visscher, A. J., & Witziers, B. (2004). Subject departments as professional communities? *British Educational Research Journal, 30*(6), 785–800.

Voelkl, K. E. (1997). Identification with school. *American Journal of Education*, *105*(3), 294–318.

Wahlstrom, K. L., & Louis, K. S. (2008). How teachers experience principal leadership: The roles of professional community, trust, efficacy, and shared responsibility. *Educational Administration Quarterly, 44*(4), 458–495.

Walker, J., & Slear, S. (2011). The impact of principal leadership behaviors on the efficacy of new and experienced middle school teachers. *NASSP Bulletin, 95*(1), 46–64.

Wayman, J., & Stringfield, S. (2006). Technology-supported involvement of entire faculties in examination of student data for instructional improvement. *American Journal of Education, 112*(4), 549–571.

Wayne, A. J., & Youngs, P. (2003). Teacher characteristics and student achievement gains: A review. *Review of Educational Research, 73*(1), 89–122.

Webb, R. (2005). Leading teaching and learning in the primary school. *Educational Management Administration & Leadership, 33*(1), 69–91.

Weinstein, R. (1976). Reading group membership in first-grade: Teacher behaviors and pupil experience over time. *Journal of Educational Psychology, 68*(1), 103–116.

Weis, L. (1990). *Working class without work: High school students in a de-industrializing economy.* New York, NY: Routledge.

Wellisch, J. B., MacQueen, A. H., Carriere, R. A., & Duck, G. A. (1978, July). School management and organization in successful schools. *Sociology of Education, 51*, 211–226.

Wenger, E. (1998). *Communities of practice: Learning, meaning, and identity.* Cambridge, England: Cambridge University Press.

Wenger, E. (2000). Communities of practice and social learning systems, Organization *7*(2), 225–246.

Wenger, E., & Snyder, W. (2000). Communities of practice: The organizational frontier. *Harvard Business Review, 78*(1), 139–146.

Wilson, B. L., & Corbett, H. (1999). *No excuses: The eighth grade year in six Philadelphia middle schools.* Philadelphia, PA: Philadelphia Education Fund.

Wilson, B. L., & Corcoran, T. B. (1988). *Successful secondary schools: Visions of excellence in American public education.* New York, NY: Falmer.

Wilson, S. M., & Berne, J. (1999). Teacher learning and the acquisition of professional knowledge: An examination of research on contemporary professional development. In A. Iran-Nejad & P. D. Pearson (Eds.), *Review of research in education* (pp. 173–209). Washington, DC: American Educational Research Association.

Witziers, B., Bosker, R. J., & Krüger, M. L. (2003). Educational leadership and student achievement: The elusive search for an association. *Educational Administration Quarterly, 39*(3), 398–425.

Wohlstetter, P., Datnow, A., & Park, V. (2008). Creating a system for data-driven decision-making: Applying the principal-agent framework. *School Effectiveness and School Improvement, 19*(3), 239–259.

Woloszyk, C. (1996). *Models for at-risk youth. Final report.* Kalamazoo, MI: Upjohn Institute for Employment Research.

Wraga, W. G. (1994). *Democracy's high school: The comprehensive high school and educational reform in the United States.* Lanham, MD: University Press of America.

Yair, G. (2000). Not just about time: Instructional practices and productive time in school. *Educational Administration Quarterly, 36*(4), 485–512.

York-Barr, J., & Duke, K. (2004). What do we know about teacher leadership? Findings from two decades of scholarship. *Review of Educational Research, 74*(3), 255–316.

Young, V. (2006). Teachers' use of data: Loose coupling, agenda setting, and team norms. *American Journal of Education, 112*(4), 521–548.

Youngs, P. (2007). How elementary principals' beliefs and actions influence new teachers' experiences. *Educational Administration Quarterly, 43*(1), 101–137.

Youngs, P., & King, M. B. (2002). Principal leadership for professional development to build school capacity. *Educational Administration Quarterly, 38*(5), 643–670.

Zaccaro, S. J., Kemp, C., & Bader, P. (2004). Leader traits and attributes. In J. Antonakis, A. T. Cianciolo, & R. J. Sternberg (Eds.), *The nature of leadership* (pp. 101–124). Thousand Oaks, CA: SAGE.

Zimpher, N. L. (1988, January/February). A design for the professional development of teacher leaders. *Journal of Teacher Education, 39*(1), 53–60.

Index

CORWIN
A SAGE Company

CORWIN HAS ONE MISSION: to enhance education through intentional professional learning.

We build long-term relationships with our authors, educators, clients, and associations who partner with us to develop and continuously improve the best evidence-based practices that establish and support lifelong learning.

Solutions you want. Experts you trust. Results you need.

Author Consulting

Author Consulting

On-site professional learning with sustainable results! Let us help you design a professional learning plan to meet the unique needs of your school or district. www.corwin.com/pd

Institutes

Institutes

Corwin Institutes provide collaborative learning experiences that equip your team with tools and action plans ready for immediate implementation. www.corwin.com/institutes

eCourses

eCourses

Practical, flexible online professional learning designed to let you go at your own pace. www.corwin.com/ecourses

Read2Earn

Read2Earn

Did you know you can earn graduate credit for reading this book? Find out how: www.corwin.com/read2earn

Contact an account manager at (800) 831-6640 or visit **www.corwin.com** for more information.